Ashbel Green, John C. Lowrie

Presbyterian missions

Ashbel Green, John C. Lowrie

Presbyterian missions

ISBN/EAN: 9783743334151

Manufactured in Europe, USA, Canada, Australia, Japa

Cover: Foto ©ninafisch / pixelio.de

Manufactured and distributed by brebook publishing software (www.brebook.com)

Ashbel Green, John C. Lowrie

Presbyterian missions

PRESBYTERIAN MISSIONS

BY

ASHBEL GREEN, D.D., LL.D.

WITH SUPPLEMENTAL NOTES

BY

JOHN C. LOWRIE

NEW YORK
ANSON D. F. RANDOLPH & COMPANY
(INCORPORATED)
182 FIFTH AVENUE

COPYRIGHT, 1893, BY
ANSON D. F. RANDOLPH & COMPANY,
(INCORPORATED).

PRESS OF
EDWARD O. JENKINS' SON,
NEW YORK.

PRESBYTERIAN MISSIONS

ADVERTISEMENT—NOTE.

The Board of Foreign Missions of the Presbyterian Church, at their meeting in Baltimore, in October and November, 1837, passed the following resolution, viz.:

"*Resolved*, That the Rev. Dr. Green be requested to draw up a history of the Foreign Missionary operations of the Presbyterian Church in the United States, to be published by the Executive Committee, with the proceedings of this Board."

When the duty assigned by the foregoing resolution came to be performed, it was found on examination, that Domestic and Foreign Missions in the Presbyterian Church had not only been conducted by the same agencies, but that, to some extent, they had been mingled together. A compendious view of both, was therefore determined on, as stated in the introduction to the Sketch.

Institutions established or conducted mainly by associations or individuals, not immediately connected with the Presbyterian Church, when mentioned at all, have received but a cursory and summary notice. Their operations have not been traced, although carried on in concert with members of the Presbyterian denomination. Institutions *characteristically Presbyterian* have been regarded as the only proper subjects of anything like historical detail. Nor has it been considered as consistent with the plan adopted, to mention such of these as were known to have had no other than a very brief existence, or a very limited action. If any societies having a just claim to be noticed in this compendious view, have been altogether omitted, the writer can only say, that they have escaped inquiries, made as extensively and diligently as his time and means of information would permit.

It is hoped that the readers of this Sketch will keep in mind that its nature forbade much enlargement. It had been easier for the author to compose a much larger work, than to condense his materials, after he had collected them, into the necessary compass. Probably some will think that equal justice has not been done to the numerous institutions that have been brought under review. This will not be fairly attributed to partiality in the writer—it is owing solely to the fact, that after much research he could obtain but scanty materials for some articles, while for others his materials were abundant, and near at hand. He is sensible of the defects of his work, but with all its imperfections he hopes it may be useful.

As this Sketch could not be submitted to the Board of Missions, and as the larger part of it has not been seen even by the Executive Committee, it is to be distinctly understood, that the writer alone is responsible for the statements it contains.—A. G.

[Dr. Green's History has long been out of print, and no book supplies its place. It contains valuable information, collected from many sources, to the year 1838. Its author, one of the eminent among our American clergymen, was born at Hanover, N. J., July 6, 1762. He graduated at Princeton College with the first honors, under the Presidency of Dr. Witherspoon, in 1783, and yielded to his preceptor's urgent counsel to accept the call of the Second Presbyterian church, Philadelphia. His ministry in this church was greatly blessed, and attended with special revivals of religion. For twenty-five years he was the pastor of this large and influential congregation; and then, with the deep regret of both parties, resigning its charge, he accepted the Presidency of Princeton College. At the end of ten years, on retiring from active public services, he became the author of valuable books and the editor for twelve years of a monthly religious magazine, the *Christian Advocate*. In some of his latter years he preached to a small congregation of colored people in Philadelphia. He was always an earnest and efficient friend of Missions. A personal interview with him in 1833 called forth expressions of deep sympathy with this cause. He departed this life May 17, 1848.

This book is here reprinted as it left the author's pen, with a few omissions specified where they occur, and with some changes not affecting its meaning, such as the transfer of foot-notes, in some cases to the text, and the removal of his Appendix to its intended place, at page 215. Corrections or omissions have been made in extracts quoted from Annual Reports, rendered proper by later information. The Supplemental Notes, distinguished by brackets [ ], are inserted usually at the dates of the narrative or the suggestions of the subject; and sometimes without close connection with the original text, but still in keeping with its purpose. These Notes have been gathered chiefly from many volumes published, or which have become accessible, since the year 1838; but in some instances they have been derived from personal knowledge. They sometimes refer to matters of later date, connected with preceding events or subjects.

The plan of this History includes three periods, viz.: First, from 1741 to 1838, embracing Domestic and Foreign Missions, both then conducted under the same direction—that of the General Assembly, or by some of the Synods. This part is treated of in this volume. Second, from 1839 to 1869. Third, from 1870 to ——. The narratives of the two latter periods will relate only to Foreign Missions. They may not soon be ready for the press; but the first volume admits of being separately published. The occasion of preparing it is found in the Minute of the Board of Foreign Missions, of February 16, 1891. This kind Minute was understood by the Editor to include a transfer from routine to special work, as Providence might indicate. Any pecuniary avails that may reach him from this book will, as heretofore, go to the cause of Missions.

J. C. L.

NEW YORK, 53 Fifth Avenue, December, 1892.]

CONTENTS.

INTRODUCTION...	1
DOMESTIC MISSIONS.......................................	2
Presbyterian Church always a missionary church..........	3
Virginia and the Carolinas early regarded as missionary ground...	3
Collections annually taken up in the Churches, by order of the Synod of New York and Philadelphia in 1766, to aid in sending the Gospel to destitute places................	4
THE GENERAL ASSEMBLY constituted 1788, and met the first time at Philadelphia, May, 1789..........................	4
Vigorous measures adopted by the General Assembly to raise funds for the missionary cause, 1800................	5
Standing Committee of Missions appointed in 1802.........	6
Circular addressed to every Protestant Missionary Society known in Europe...	7
Missionary operations among the African race in the Southern section of our country...............................	7
Services performed by the lamented John H. Rice, D.D...	8
Synod of Virginia instrumental in forming Presbyterian churches in Kentucky.....................................	9
Synod of Pittsburgh efficiently engaged in sustaining Foreign and Domestic Missions................................	9
Monthly periodical issued by the Standing Committee of the General Assembly.......................................	9
WESTERN FOREIGN MISSIONARY SOCIETY OF NEW JERSEY, formed in 1800. Its organization independent of the General Assembly...	9
BOARD OF MISSIONS OF THE GENERAL ASSEMBLY, constituted in 1816..	10
Formation of Missionary Societies auxiliary to the General Assembly's Board recommended........................	10
Duties of Secretary and General Agent of the Board of Missions performed by a few of the members, amidst pastoral and other engagements............................	11

CONTENTS.

Young Men's Missionary Society of New York, formed 1815. ... 11
New York Evangelical Missionary Society, instituted about 1816 ... 12
United Domestic Missionary Society, formed by the union of the Young Men's Missionary Society and the New York Evangelical Missionary Society. ... 12
Meeting of delegates from different States of New-England held at Boston, in 1826, to form a General Society for Domestic Missions. ... 13
American Home Missionary Society, instituted May, 1826.. 14
Refusal of the American Home Missionary Society to cooperate with the General Assembly's Board of Missions. 14
Resolution of the General Assembly of 1837, recommending the discontinuance of the operations of the American Home Missionary Society and the American Education Society within the Presbyterian Church. ... 15
The organization of a Philadelphia Missionary and other Presbyterian Missionary Societies in the city and liberties of Philadelphia. ... 17
Pennsylvania Missionary Society, formed 1826. ... 18
Re-organization of the Board of Missions of the General Assembly in 1828. ... 19

FOREIGN OR HEATHEN MISSIONS. ... 22
Indian Mission on Long Island, the first heathen mission instituted in the Presbyterian Church. ... 23
Second mission under Rev. David Brainerd. ... 24
Mission to Indians in eastern Pennsylvania, eastern New York, and New Jersey. ... 24
Rev. John Brainerd succeeds his brother. ... 28
New York Missionary Society, organized 1796. ... 30
Transfer of all their missions to the United Foreign Missionary Society. ... 31
Northern Missionary Society, organized 1797. ... 31
Mission to the Cherokee Indians. ... 32
Rev. Gideon Blackburn engaged as a missionary. ... 33
Efforts to establish schools among the Cherokees. ... 33
Letter from Rev. G. Blackburn on the progress of civilization among the Indians. ... 34

CONTENTS.   xi

Mission among the Wyandot Indians	35
Mission at Cornplanter's Town	36
Mission at Lewistown, Ohio	38
United Foreign Missionary Society instituted 1818	38
Their operations countenanced and patronized by the general government	40
The Two Osage Missions	42
The want of success in this mission induces its final abandonment	43
The Cattaraugus Mission	44
Encouraging circumstances connected with it	45
The Mackinaw Mission	45
The Hayticn Mission	46
The Tuscarora Mission	47
The Seneca Mission	49
Legislature of New York reject a petition praying for the residence of ministers of the Gospel on Indian lands	49
The Fort Gratiot Mission	50
The Maumee Mission	50
Proceedings of the Synod of Pittsburgh in relation thereto	51
Report on the state of the Maumee school	52
Remarks on the transfer of the missions of the United Foreign Missionary Society to the American Board	54
Reasons adduced in favor of this union	55
Remarks on the preceding reasons	58
Action of the General Assembly and Synod of the Reformed Dutch Church, on the subject of the amalgamation	60
Report and resolution of the General Assembly	63
Mission among the Chickasaw Indians, the only one in the Presbyterian Church, not transferred to the American Board	65
Chickasaw Mission under the supervision of the Synod of South Carolina and Georgia	65
Foreign and Domestic Missions authorized by the General Assembly	84
Mission to Buenos Ayres	85
Resolution of the General Assembly's Board of Missions rendering assistance to this mission	87
Cause of failure	88, 89

CONTENTS.

Concluding remarks on the different sentiments existing in the Presbyterian Church on the most eligible method of prosecuting Foreign Missions.......................... 89

WESTERN FOREIGN MISSIONARY SOCIETY FORMED IN NOVEMBER, 1831... 101
    Circular letter issued by this Society..................... 101
    Formation of the Society..................... 103
    Extracts from the Life of the Rev. Joseph W. Barr, one of its missionaries 112
    Missions and missionaries under the care of the Western Foreign Missionary Society 112

MISSION TO WESTERN AFRICA............ 114
    Ordination of Missionaries....................... 114
    Death of the Rev. Joseph W. Barr, one of the missionaries destined for Africa............................ 115
    Embarkation of Missionaries........................... 116
    Their arrival at Monrovia 116
    Death of Mr. Cloud and Mr. and Mrs. Laird............. 117
    The state of the African Mission....................... 120

MISSION TO NORTHERN INDIA............................. 126
    Embarkation and arrival of the Missionaries............. 127
    Death of Mrs. Lowrie.... 128
    Death of Mr. Reed 142
    Reinforcement of the Mission by the arrival of several Missionaries... 143
    Mr. Lowrie has permission to return to the United States to recruit his health...................................... 156
    Details of the three missionary stations in Northern India.. 163

MISSION TO THE WESTERN INDIANS....................... 165

THE IOWA MISSION....................................... 169
    Details of the *Wea* and *Iowa* stations.................... 171

MISSION TO SMYRNA..................................... 171

MISSION TO CHINA....................................... 173
    Interesting statement relative to the progress of casting types of the Chinese characters........................ 175

PROJECTED OR PROSPECTIVE MISSIONS.................... 179

INDIAN TRIBES... 180

MISSION TO CALCUTTA..... 182

THE FOREIGN MISSIONARY CHRONICLE.................... 184

CONTENTS.

TRANSFER OF THE WESTERN FOREIGN MISSIONARY SOCIETY.. 189
 Proceedings of the General Assembly of 1835, in relation to the transfer.................................... 190
 Report of a Committee to the General Assembly of 1836... 190
 Terms of agreement between the Committee of the General Assembly and the Synod of Pittsburgh................ 192
 Report of a Committee appointed by the General Assembly of 1836, to review the whole case, and present it to the consideration of the Assembly....................... 195
 Proceedings of the Assembly on the report, and final rejection thereof.. 200
 Transactions in General Assembly of 1837............... 221
 Report of the Committee on the overture from the Presbytery of Salem, on the subject of foreign missions, and of "The Board of Foreign Missions of the Presbyterian Church in the United States of America"............... 221
 Directors for the Board of Foreign Missions appointed..... 223
 First meeting of the Board held October, 1837........... 226
 Proceedings of the Western Foreign Missionary Society, at its last Meeting, May, 1837........................... 214

CONCLUDING REMARKS... 220
 1. The importance of sustaining our missionary operations on right principles, and from right motives............ 230
 2. Before the world shall be converted to God, there must be a practical conviction that it is the power of God alone, working on the minds of the heathen, that can ever change them.................................... 232
 3. Dependence on God for the success of missions ought not to diminish, but increase, the means and exertions that are used to produce this effect................... 235
 4. Faithful missionaries ought to be "esteemed very highly in love for their work's sake," and every reasonable provision made for their support in foreign lands......... 239
 5. We ought not to calculate that great and speedy success will follow our missionary enterprises................ 239
 6. Strict economy ought to be observed in the use of funds in managing the missionary concerns at home........ 240

APPENDICES... 243
 I. Presbyterian Missionaries........................... 243
 II. Books of Reference.................................. 246

INDEX OF SUPPLEMENTARY NOTES................................ 247

A HISTORICAL SKETCH

OF

PRESBYTERIAN MISSIONS.

INTRODUCTION.

THE propagation of the Gospel in North America possessed, essentially, the character of a Missionary enterprise. Its propagators when they fled from persecution in the land of their fathers, had it in view, not only to be able to worship God according to the dictates of their consciences, free from molestation, but to transmit the Gospel in its purity to their descendants, and to other emigrants, in all succeeding generations; and they also hoped to impart its blessings to the Pagan tribes, who inhabited the wilderness in which they sought an abode. As introductory, therefore, to a brief "History of the Foreign Missionary Operations of the Presbyterian Church in the United States," it is proposed to take a rapid survey of the Missions of this Church among the descendants of Europeans; and to follow it by a narrative, more in detail, of missionary operations, among the aborigines of our own country, and among the heathen of foreign lands. It is believed that the present will not be considered as an unfit occasion for the survey contemplated; nor prove unwelcome to those who take an interest in the concerns of the Presbyterian Church, many of whom are almost wholly unacquainted with its missionary history.

DOMESTIC MISSIONS.

THE Presbytery of Philadelphia was the first that existed on the American continent, and was formed, as nearly as can be ascertained, in the year 1704. Its clerical members were emigrants from Scotland and Ireland, with one individual from New England. They were, with a single exception, almost wholly destitute of property; and the people to whom they ministered, being like themselves in poverty, and struggling for subsistence in a wilderness land, could contribute but a pittance to the support of their pastors.

In these circumstances, little more could be done for spreading the Gospel, than to proclaim its truths and administer its ordinances, among the inhabitants in the vicinity of the preachers. But in this field of operation, the labors of the fathers of the Presbyterian Church were most exemplary. It may be questioned whether any missionaries, in more recent times, have made greater exertions to carry the Gospel to the destitute, or have endured more hardships in doing it, than were exhibited by these venerable and devoted men. They not only preached to the people to whom they sustained the pastoral relation, but extended, as far as possible, their excursions of benevolence into the adjacent regions; and this without any pecuniary compensation or facilities of travelling. The affecting cries of the destitute came to them at every meeting of their Presbytery, as well as at their individual abodes; and the efforts which they made to relieve the spiritual wants of the suppliants, were neither few nor feeble.

In process of time, when the Presbytery was enlarged into a Synod, and a small fund was obtained to aid the operations, and partially to relieve the pressing necessities of its members, missionary services were extended to places more remote. It was in this way that Presbyterian churches were planted, not only in the British colonies of Pennsylvania and Maryland, but also in Virginia, and in North and South Carolina. The Presbyterian Church has, in fact, been always a Missionary Church; and to her being such, is to be attributed, under the blessing of God, her rapid increase and her present wide extension. In a period of little more than a hundred and thirty years, this Church, embracing at first but six or seven ministers of the Gospel, has located congregations, with their pastors, through a region extending from Canada, on the North, to Florida, in the South, and from the Atlantic, on the East, to parts beyond the Mississippi, in the West; and now consists of nineteen Synods, one hundred and six Presbyteries, and nearly two thousand ordained ministers; between two and three hundred licentiates; more than two hundred and forty candidates for the Gospel ministry; and not less than two thousand churches. Of the *detail* of her Domestic Missions, only the most cursory view can now be taken.

It has already been stated, that Virginia and the Carolinas were early regarded as missionary ground; and we now add, that they continued to be thus regarded, till the commencement of the Revolutionary war of our country. Their necessities formed a marked subject of attention, and measures were adopted for their relief, at almost every meeting of the Synod, before the unhappy rent which divided it, in 1741. After that occurrence, till the reunion of the Synods in 1758, each of the conflicting bodies made vigorous exertions to supply the spiritual wants of the southern portion of the then British colonies. The result was, that not only many churches were organized, but several Presbyteries were formed in that section of our country.

In the year 1766, the Synod of New York and Philadelphia, then the supreme judicatory of the Church, directed that a subscription should be taken up, or a collection made, in all their congregations, vacant as well as supplied, for sending the Gospel to destitute places; and, in the following year, they determined that such a collection should be annually made; and they adopted other suitable measures to carry into effect their benevolent design.

During the war of Independence, the public mind was so engrossed with the state of the country that all religious institutions languished, and some were temporarily suspended. In the South, the hostile armies overran, and for a time had the occupancy of a part of the region, to which missions had previously been sent; and missionary operations, on the whole frontier of the United States, were precluded, by the existence or the fear of Indian hostilities. Such, nevertheless, was the strength of the missionary spirit in the Presbyterian Church, that a number of missionaries were sent forth during this war; and the subject continued to command the serious attention of the Synod of New York and Philadelphia, as long as it remained the highest judicatory of the Presbyterian Church. The General Assembly, which was constituted by that Synod in 1788, met, for the first time, in Philadelphia, in May, 1789. During the sessions of this first year, the missionary cause claimed a particular attention. The four Synods, then existing under the Assembly, were directed to provide and recommend, each, two missionaries to the next Assembly; and that funds might be prepared to meet the expense expected to be incurred, it was enjoined on all the Presbyteries, to take measures for raising collections, in all the congregations within their bounds.

It is believed that at this time (1789) there was not, in the United States, another religious denomination beside the Presbyterian, that prosecuted any domestic missionary enterprise; except that then, as since, the Methodists sent forth their circuit riders, in various directions. A few years subsequently, the Congregationalists of Connecticut sent missionaries among the emigrants from that State, who had located themselves within the bounds of the States of New York and Pennsylvania; and, in Massachusetts also, at a period somewhat later, missionary operations were set on foot. But for some time, with the exception stated, the Presbyterian Church stood alone, at least as to any regular and systematic efforts, in supplying the destitute portions of our country with the preaching of the Gospel. For thirteen years in succession, the General Assembly, at every annual meeting, either by a committee appointed for the purpose, or by measures adopted on motion in the House, took the missionary concern into special consideration, heard the reports of those appointed in a preceding year, and made new appointments, as extensively as missionaries and the means of their support could be obtained.

In 1800, measures of increased vigor and efficiency were adopted, to raise funds for the support of the missionary cause. Agents were commissioned and sent out into different parts of the country, to solicit donations in aid of the Assembly's Missions; and the result was, the formation of a fund of upwards of twenty-two thousand dollars, conditioned by the donors, that the capital should remain unbroken, and the annual interest only be expended. At this period, the Rev. Jedediah Chapman was appointed a stated missionary for four years, in the northwestern part of the State of New York; to direct and assist other missionaries, and to spend six months of each year in personal labors, in this, at that time, the most favored missionary field. He subsequently received missionary appointments, till the time of his death in 1813. The same year (1800) the Rev. James Hall was appointed a missionary to Natchez, for several months; and was accompanied by the Rev. James Bowman and William Montgomery, appointed by the Synod of the Carolinas. This mission was performed in a very able and satisfactory manner.

In 1802, an important alteration took place in the manner of conducting the Missionary business. It had now become so extensive, that the Assembly found it would be impossible, amidst the numerous concerns claiming their attention, to devote to it, during the short term of their annual sessions, that time and regard which its successful and extended prosecution demanded. To diminish their business, and to ensure a proper management of all their missionary affairs, they appointed a Standing Committee of Missions, to act through the year; prescribed to them the duties to be performed, and clothed them with such powers as were then deemed sufficient. Immediately on the rising of the Assembly, the Committee organized themselves, and entered with alacrity and zeal on the discharge of the interesting duties assigned them. A circular letter was addressed to Presbyteries, urging their assistance in the missionary enterprise; a system of instructions was drawn up and printed, for directing the conduct of the missionaries employed; and a circular letter was prepared and sent by the Committee to every Protestant Missionary Society known to exist in Europe—containing information in regard to missionary operations in our country at large, and more particularly in our own Church. A series of questions on missionary concerns was also contained in the letter, and answers were solicited, from which it was hoped that much useful information might be derived, to aid the Committee in the management of their important business. Due attention was paid to this letter, by the Societies to which it was addressed, and numerous and friendly replies were received. Under the conduct of the Committee, the Missionary operations became more and more extensive; and the satisfaction was enjoyed of beholding them constantly exerting a most benign influence on the cause of religion. In one year of its existence, the Committee recommended, and the Assembly sanctioned, fifty-one missionary appointments.

It ought to be particularly noted, that a very zealous effort was made by the Standing Committee to establish regular missionary operations among the unhappy African race, in the southern section of our country. With this view, they commissioned the Rev. John Chavis, a man of African descent, who had previously been employed as a missionary among the blacks, by the Synod of Virginia. From the General Assembly, on the recommendation of the Committee, he received, for six years in succession, missionary appointments to the people of his color, in Virginia and North Carolina. Nor did he labor altogether in vain.

[The brief reference to Mr. Chavis in the text may be supplemented by later information. He was a negro of full blood, but a freeman. He was born in 1763, near Oxford, N. C., and educated at Princeton College, under Dr. Witherspoon. His expenses were defrayed by gentlemen in the neighborhood of Oxford, who wished to see how far a negro could be well educated. He was licensed as a preacher by a New Jersey Presbytery, and accompanied the Rev. Samuel Davis to Virginia, where he engaged in the work of the ministry. In that State he preached the Gospel acceptably until 1805, and then was transferred to North Carolina, where he continued in faithful work in three counties, one of them his native county, until 1832. He died in 1838, in his seventy-fifth year. He was aided in his later years by the Presbytery for his support, which was continued to his widow. His ministry was eminently useful, and for several years he conducted a classical school for white boys. This school was considered the best in the State at that time. Many eminent professional men, sons of the best families in the State, received their education in it; some of whom were still living a few years ago, who spoke in warm terms of praise of their former teacher. The great respect and kindly feeling which were shown to Mr. Chavis were due to his own character and life, and were worthy not only of himself, but of his white friends. His memoirs should be accessible, for the benefit of his race, and not less of white people, both in our Northern and Southern States. It is our blessed religion that must mainly solve existing and grave difficulties.*]

But the most important and efficient services, in this field of benevolent action, were performed by the late eminent and lamented John H. Rice, D.D. For seven

* This imperfect note is abridged from an article in the Chicago *Interior* of April 28, 1892, written by a respected minister of the Southern Presbyterian Church.

years he cheerfully accepted a mission to the black population of Virginia, and labored among them with the most exemplary fidelity and happy success. The fruits of his mission are said to be yet visible, and to be remembered with gratitude, by a number of those to whom his labors were blessed.

But beside the missionaries commissioned by the Assembly, a considerable number were annually sent forth by the Synods, who managed this interesting concern separately from the Assembly. The Synods of the Carolinas, Virginia, Kentucky, and Pittsburgh, were distinguished for their zeal and efficiency in the missionary cause. By the missionary operations of the Synod of Virginia, some of the first Presbyterian churches in Kentucky were formed, and afterwards supplied with the Gospel ordinances. But of all the Synods, that of Pittsburgh was the longest and most extensively and efficiently engaged in sustaining missions, both domestic and foreign.

It ought not to be omitted, that among the other labors of the Standing Committee of Missions, was the distribution of a large number of religious books and tracts, and the editing and publishing of a monthly Miscellany of fifty octavo pages.

In a compendious view of Missions in the Presbyterian Church, some notice is due to "The Western Missionary Society of New Jersey." It was formed about the year 1800. Its organization, indeed, was entirely independent of the General Assembly. But it was composed of members belonging to the same church, contributed liberally to the funds of the Assembly, pursued the same objects, and was, for a length of time, active and spirited in the execution of its own missionary plans. Its operations ceased, principally for the want of funds, about four years since.

In 1816, the Standing Committee of Missions, on their own recommendation, was succeeded by a Board, which, by an order of the Assembly, was styled "The Board of Missions acting under the authority of the General Assembly of the Presbyterian Church in the United States." The powers of the Committee had not extended beyond the nomination of missionaries to the Assembly, pointing out their routes of travel or fields of labor, and specifying the amount of salary due to each. A final action on all these points was among the powers now granted to this Board; whose members were not confined to Philadelphia and its vicinity, but were taken, in part, from each of the Synods composing the Assembly —to which body an annual report of all the transactions of the preceding year was required to be made. The centre of action was still in Philadelphia. The Assembly "authorized and directed the Board to take measures for establishing throughout the churches, Auxiliary Missionary Societies, and recommended to their people the establishment of such societies, to aid the funds and extend the operations of the Board." In carrying this order of the Assembly into effect, the Board recommended the formation of Auxiliary Societies in every Presbytery, and the formation of Missionary Associations, as far as practicable, in all the congregations of each Presbytery; and, to a considerable extent, this recommendation was complied with. For a time, the operations of this Board were prosecuted with much vigor, and an encouraging success. And although in no year did the Board commission as many missionaries as had been recommended to the Assembly, in some years of the Standing Committee, to which it succeeded, yet for a series of years its efficiency was great, in conveying widely the blessings of the Gospel to the destitute.

It deserves especial notice, that in almost every part of our country, numerous infant churches were organized by the travelling missionaries of this Board, which could not otherwise have been formed; and which afterwards furnished the opportunity, so happily embraced by other institutions, to afford assistance, in the support of their pastors or stated supplies. But for a considerable period before its reorganization, the Board languished greatly; and all its operations were crippled and circumscribed by the want of funds. Other institutions came in conflict with applications for supplies, from the sources whence they had previously been derived. In a word, it became evident, that if some effective measures were not speedily taken to reanimate the Board, it would soon either cease to exist, or exist in nothing but name. Neither this Board, nor the Standing Committee which preceded it, had ever employed a Corresponding Secretary and General Agent, nor appointed an Executive Committee. All their duties were discharged by a few of their members, the clerical part of whom were constantly occupied, with numerous pastoral engagements.

YOUNG MEN'S SOCIETY OF NEW YORK. The Young Men's Missionary Society of New York was formed in the city of New York, as nearly as the writer has been able to ascertain, in the year 1815; and was laudably active for a number of years, in supplying the destitute portions of that State, and, to some extent, the contiguous parts of the States of Pennsylvania and New Jersey, with the preaching of the Gospel. The last report which they made, while they existed as a distinct organization, states that in the preceding year they had employed nine missionaries, whose labors had not only been highly acceptable, but in some instances greatly blessed.

NEW YORK EVANGELICAL SOCIETY. The New York Evangelical Missionary Society appears to have been instituted about a year (1816) subsequently to the one last mentioned. In the conclusion of their fifth and last annual report, in December, 1821, they say: "In summing up the operations of the Board, it appears that they had in their employment the present year ten missionaries—one in the State of Missouri, six in the middle and western counties of New York, one on Long Island, and two in the city of New York. To support these operations, considerable funds were required, and much has been generously bestowed." The colored people of New York City received a particular attention from this Society, and a colored missionary whom they employed, appears to have been blessed in his ministrations.

UNITED DOMESTIC SOCIETY. The two Societies last mentioned, as appears by what follows, were merged in "The United Domestic Missionary Society." This Society, says an authentic document, "was organized on the 9th of May, 1822, by a Convention of delegates from Domestic Missionary Associations in various parts of the State of New York. Soon after its organization two respectable Domestic Missionary Societies in this city (New York), having twenty-eight missionaries under their care, transferred their concerns to this new institution." It was only for about four years that this institution acted under the name or title which it assumed at its origin. But during this period its operations were carried on with energy and success. Many auxiliary societies were established; and the number of missionaries which it employed increased from seventy-five in the first year to one hundred and twenty-one in the year before it changed its name. The success of its missionaries, moreover, was represented as most decisive and encouraging. The State of New York, in which the Society originated, shared largely, but not exclusively, in the labors of its missionaries. The destitution of Gospel ordinances in the newly-formed States of the West attracted the particular attention of the Society; but no itinerating missionaries were employed. On the contrary, they were denounced as a nuisance to the Church; and the building up of feeble churches, so as to establish a settled ministry in them, was avowedly the exclusive plan of this Society.

AMERICAN HOME MISSIONARY SOCIETY. A meeting of delegates from the different States of New England was held at Boston, in an early part of the year 1826, at which the formation of a General Society for Domestic Missions was recommended, the seat of which should be at New York. Apprised of this, the Executive Committee of the United Domestic Missionary Society invited the directors of that Association, together with other friends of missions in the United States, "to convene at the session room of the Brick Presbyterian Church in that city, on Wednesday, the tenth day of May, at eight o'clock, A.M., for the purpose of forming an American Home Missionary Society." This Convention was accordingly held at the time designated; and after some preliminary proceedings, "the Rev. Mr. Peters, Corresponding Secretary of the United Domestic Missionary Society, read a form of a Constitution, which the Executive Committee had agreed to recommend to the Convention"; after which the following resolution was passed: "That this Convention entirely approve of the proposed plan of a National Home Missionary Society, and that they will now proceed to consider the Constitution that has been offered."

After considering the Constitution, the Convention adopted the following resolutions:

"That this Convention approve the proposed Constitution, and recommend to the United Domestic Missionary Society to adopt the same, and to become the American Home Missionary Society."

"That the officers of this meeting be a Committee of the Convention, to present to the United Domestic Missionary Society a statement of the proceedings of this meeting, together with the proposed Constitution, and the preceding recommendation that the same be adopted. On the Friday evening following, the United Domestic Missionary Society met for the adoption of the Constitution, as recommended by the Convention." * Such was the origin of the American Home Missionary Society.

This Society consisted, when organized, of various distinct ecclesiastical bodies, or associations, three-fourths of which were not Presbyterian; and it acknowledged no responsibility to any judicatory of the Presbyterian Church. It refused, although kindly invited, to co-operate in missionary concerns with the Assembly's Board, but came forth against it in open hostility, and labored for some years to thwart its operations and destroy its influence. It was never denied that this Society, especially in the early periods of its existence, had in its connection many estimable members of the Presbyterian Church, was instrumental in building up and supplying with pastors no inconsiderable number of feeble congregations in this Church, and that on this account it for a time received the countenance of the General Assembly.

But it was not long before it became palpably evident

---

* See *Missionary Herald*, vol. xxii., pp. 161, 191.

that in every conflict in the General Assembly, in which an attempt was made to sustain discipline or to maintain in their integrity the doctrines and government of the Church, the attempt was resisted, and in general defeated, by the friends and dependents of this Society. In a word, it became notorious, that the unhappy and reproachful distractions of the Church, threatening not only its peace but its very existence, were attributable, in a great measure, to the influence of this institution; in introducing as pastors, and consequently as members of Presbyteries, and ultimately as members of the General Assembly, men of unsound theological opinions, and nearly always of lax sentiments, in regard to the government and discipline of the Church; and that, of course, peace and order could not be restored till this evil should be abated. Under this conviction, the General Assembly of 1837 passed the following resolution:

"*Resolved,* That while we desire that no body of Christian men of other denominations should be prevented from choosing their own plans of doing good; and while we claim no right to complain, should they exceed us in energy and zeal—we believe that facts too familiar to need repetition here, warrant us in affirming that the organization and operations of the so-called American Home Missionary Society and American Education Society, and its branches of whatever name, are exceedingly injurious to the peace and purity of the Presbyterian Church. We recommend, accordingly, that they should cease to operate within our churches."

Any Christian Church will be preponderantly influenced, and will eventually find all its important measures moulded and directed by those who conduct the education or training of its youth for the Gospel ministry;

and who possess, at the same time, the exclusive management of its domestic and foreign missions. The truth of this position will not be doubted by any intelligent person, who candidly and carefully considers the nature of the case, and who is able and willing to consult and appreciate the evidence derivable from observation and experience. Let it then be observed, that the American Education Society, the American Home Missionary Society, and the American Board of Commissioners for Foreign Missions, if their views had been carried into full effect, would in fact have conducted, to a great and commanding extent, if not exclusively, the education or training of youth for the Gospel ministry in the Presbyterian Church; and would, at the same time, have directed all the Domestic and Foreign Missions of that Church. Now, it is known that all these institutions are without any ecclesiastical organization or responsibility whatever; and yet, in the case supposed, they would have possessed a preponderant influence in the Presbyterian Church, and have given shape and direction to its most important measures. That is, the management of the concerns of this Church would have passed out of the Church (not in form but yet in fact) into the hands of secular institutions—of secular institutions, moreover, a majority of whose members, to say the least, had no partiality for Presbyterian government, usages, or creeds. It will not follow from this that those who planned the Societies in question had hostile designs against the Presbyterian Church. This the present writer neither affirms nor believes. Good men have often formed plans, or acted a part, the mischievous results of which they did not foresee, or suspect to be possible—a truth abundantly confirmed by the history of the Church in past ages.

It belongs not to the design of this sketch to speak directly of other than missionary concerns. But it may with truth be remarked, that the education of youth for the Gospel ministry is essentially connected with the subject of Missions. These youth must, many of them, be ultimately the missionaries of the Church. They form, as it were, the very elements of all missionary operations; and every friend to missions, and indeed every enlightened member of the Presbyterian Church, must regard its Board of Education as intimately and directly connected with all the best interests of the Church, and yield it accordingly a cheerful and liberal patronage.

As in New York, so also in Philadelphia, there were several Missionary Societies, which were eventually combined, and formed into a single Institution. The *Christian Advocate* for the month of April, 1826, contained, on this subject, the following statement:

"Many years ago a Philadelphia Missionary Society was organized in this city, to which each annual subscriber paid five dollars, and each subscriber for life fifty dollars. For a considerable time, it was prosperous and efficient; being able constantly to support a laborer in the metropolis and its vicinity, and sometimes to send missionaries to distant parts of the Commonwealth. Unhappily, however, the love of novelty, or some cause less commendable, produced within the last eight years four or five other Presbyterian Missionary Societies in the city and liberties of Philadelphia. This distracted the minds of our fellow-citizens, divided their resources, and paralyzed their exertions. These societies, for the most part, were supported by the same individuals; and consumed in their management five hours, where one would have been sufficient, had they been united. To produce, if possible, a better state of things, in the Presbyterian portion of this community, two of our Missionary Societies resolved to become extinct; and on the 7th of the present month, a number of gentlemen of this city resolved to co-operate with each other, in an association which is called the Pennsylvania Missionary Society.

PENNSYLVANIA MISSIONARY SOCIETY. "More than nine hundred dollars, stipulated to be paid annually, were at once subscribed by fourteen individuals, and the subscriptions of a few other persons since, have made the annual income of the Society already exceed one thousand dollars. This, we trust, will prove but a good beginning; and we earnestly entreat our Christian friends, and especially the ministers and elders of the Presbyterian Church throughout the State, to unite with us; and not to relax their exertions, until every vacant congregation in Pennsylvania has a well-informed and faithful pastor; and every town and village a dwelling-place for the Most High. The object of this Society is, to employ regular ministers of the Gospel, or licentiates of the Presbyterian or Reformed Dutch Church in the United States, to preach among the destitute in this city and State; and when their funds will allow, to assist infant churches in this and neighboring States, in maintaining the stated ministrations of the word and other ordinances of Christ. . . . . Every benevolent heart must wish success to this newly organized Society, which seems destined particularly to promote the spiritual welfare of the Presbyterian portion of this Commonwealth. The Reformed Dutch Church in this country is in all respects Presbyterian, in its creed and character; and therefore the two denominations united in this laudable enterprise can harmonize in their operations."

This Society was zealous, active, and successful, in prosecuting the objects for which it was instituted. But it did not long continue its operations; for after the reorganization of the Assembly's Board of Missions, it was seen that the very purposes for which the Society had been formed, were embraced in the plan of that Board; and therefore that the continuance of the Society would be rather injurious than useful.

Thus it appears, that while the American Home Missionary Society absorbed all the small domestic institutions of a missionary character, within the scope of its influence, the same effect was produced, on similar institutions of a strictly Presbyterian character, in the vicinity of the Missionary Board of the General Assembly. The friends of these two large and commanding bodies threw their funds and their influence into the one or the other of them, according as they were led by their predilections or their sense of duty.

In 1828 a printed Overture, signed by three clergymen and two laymen, was introduced into the Assembly, through the Committee of Overtures, proposing and urging a new organization of the Board of Missions. After an ardent and protracted debate, occasioned by opposition to the Overture by the friends of the Home Missionary Society, the Assembly resolved, "That the Board of Missions already have the power to establish Missions, not only among the destitute of our own country, or any other country, but also among the heathen in any part of the world; to select, appoint, and commission missionaries; to determine their salaries, and to settle and pay their accounts; that they have full authority to correspond with any other body on the subject of missions; to appoint an Executive Committee, and an efficient agent or agents, to manage their missionary concerns; to take measures to form auxiliary societies, on such terms as they may deem proper; to procure funds, and in general to manage the missionary operations of the General Assembly. It is therefore submitted to the discretion of the Board of Missions, to consider whether it is expedient for them to carry into effect the full powers which they possess."

THE GENERAL ASSEMBLY BOARD OF MISSIONS. No time was lost, after the rising of the Assembly, in reorganizing the Board of Missions of the General Assembly of the Presbyterian Church. At the first meeting of this Board, an Executive Committee was appointed, a Corresponding Secretary and General Agent was chosen, and the performance of the various duties of the Board was entered on, with spirit and energy. The manner in which the plans of this Board have been, and still are, carried into effect, through the agency and co-operation of Presbyteries and Sessions, and indeed the whole detail of its proceedings, are so well known throughout the Presbyterian Church, that it seemed not only unnecessary, but improper, to make a particular statement of them in this compendious view; yet it should be noted that for several years it had to contend, as already stated, with open and active opposition, from a rival institution. But its onward progress has been constant and cheering; till by its report to the General Assembly in May, 1837, it appears that in the preceding year, the Missionary Fund had amounted to nearly thirty-one thousand dollars; that the number of missionaries and agents employed had been two hundred and seventy-five; that several missionaries had been sent to places where no churches or congregations had been previously organized; that their missionaries had labored in twenty of the States of the American Union, and that the amount of ministerial labor performed, had been equal to one hundred and twenty-seven years; that the number of members added to the churches under the care of the missionaries, by examination and certificate, had been two thousand six hundred and sixty; that eighteen new churches had been organized, and about sixty houses for public worship erected; that the number of Sabbath-schools that had been formed was a little short of five hundred, in which were employed two thousand eight hundred teachers, and twelve thousand scholars; that two hundred and fifty Bible-classes had been reported, containing more than five thousand learners; that the number of Temperance Societies reported had been about three hundred and eighty, containing forty thousand members; that beside the monthly concert, four hundred weekly prayer-meetings had been established, one hundred and twenty Bible Societies, sixty-eight Tract Societies, one hundred and thirty Missionary Societies, and societies for promoting other benevolent operations in similar proportion.

Domestic Missions in the Presbyterian Church may now be considered as systematically and permanently established, and under the continued blessing of the Great Head of the Church, with every prospect of extensive and increasing usefulness.

FOREIGN OR HEATHEN MISSIONS.

AS already stated, Heathen Missions, in the infancy of the Presbyterian Church, were impracticable. It was with difficulty, and principally by their own labor and management, that the ministers of the Gospel obtained a bare subsistence for themselves and their families. The heathen in their neighborhoods lived by the chase and led an unsettled life; so that without some pecuniary aid, derived from a foreign source, a missionary could not exist among them—if indeed a missionary to them ought, in any event, to have been employed, when on all sides their own countrymen were perishing for lack of knowledge. Early, however, they found the means and the men for the prosecution of Heathen Missions. The Church of Scotland was their mother Church; and to her they looked, to enable them to send the Gospel to the pagans of the wilderness. "The Society in Scotland for propagating Christian knowledge" was instituted, in Edinburgh, in 1709. This Society, in 1741, established a Board of Correspondents in New York, who, on proper recommendation, appointed the Rev. Azariah Horton, a member of the Presbytery of New York, to labor as a missionary on Long Island, where a large number of Indians then resided. This was the first formal heathen mission, instituted in the Presbyterian Church. Whatever Christian instruction had been previously given by Presbyterian ministers to the natives of the forest, had been imparted to such as were found willing to receive it, in the neighborhood of settled pastors. Mr. Horton received from Scotland a salary of forty pounds sterling per annum; and he chose for his assistant and interpreter a man by the name of Miranda, an Indian, and formerly a trader, but who had for some time labored to instruct the Delaware and Susquehanna Indians. Mr. Horton's interpreter died, not long after his appointment, but the mission was still prosecuted by himself; and at the East end of the Island, where the greatest number of Indians were found, his success, for a time, was highly encouraging. A general reformation of manners speedily appeared, and several gave satisfactory evidence of a saving conversion; a number were taught to read, and in two or three years he had baptized forty-five adults and forty-four children. The introduction of spirituous liquors, the bane of the Indians, had an unhappy influence, in arresting the progress of the Gospel among them. Yet it appears, that so late as 1788, the Indians in those places where Mr. Horton labored were still religiously disposed, had two preachers among them, both Indians, who were well esteemed; and that a number of individuals were then in the full communion of the Church.

[The "large number of Indians" on Long Island, to whom Mr. Horton ministered, occupied a tract of country near Southampton. Their successors still remain in the same district, but are reduced in number and otherwise much changed. They are known as the Shinnecock Indians, and thirty communicants are reported in their church, in the Minutes of the General Assembly, 1892. Under date of September 10, 1891, their pastor gave the following account of them:

"Our present generation, descended from the Shinnecock tribe, is now greatly mixed with negro and Anglo-

Saxon blood, the former to much the most extent. Only two claim to be of pure Indian blood, and one hundred and sixty-two are of mixed blood. Together they make 164 persons in 34 families. Besides those who reside here, there are 96 others who do not live here, but are of the same stock, making in all 254 persons. Their temporal circumstances are not very favorable, though much better than formerly, and the future promises better still. Twenty years ago they were decreasing; for the last decade they have rapidly increased. I find them docile and kind, though not as industrious as I wish them."]

DAVID BRAINERD. The second Presbyterian missionary to the Indians was the justly celebrated David Brainerd. He also received a salary from the same Society in Scotland, by which Mr. Horton had been supported. He was licensed to preach by an association of Congregational ministers, convened at Danbury in Connecticut, July 29, 1742; and in the character of a licentiate, spent about a year in missionary labor, at an Indian settlement called Kaunaumeek, about twenty miles from Albany, in the Province of New York. Here his success was not encouraging, and his sufferings, both mental and bodily, were extreme. Inflexibly determined, however, to devote his life to the evangelizing of the heathen, he refused a pressing invitation to a very advantageous settlement, in an English congregation on Long Island. He was ordained as a missionary by the Presbytery of New York, at Newark in New Jersey, June 12, 1744. From this time to his death (October 9, 1747) he was a member both of the Presbytery and Synod of New York, and attended all their meetings, unless prevented by sickness, or by his missionary engagements. Immediately after his ordination, his attention was directed to three collections, or bodies of Indians, considerably remote from each other: namely, to those located at the forks of the Delaware River, in the Province of Pennsylvania, to those on the borders of the Susquehanna River, in the same Province, and to those who resided at a place, the Indian name of which was Crosweeksung, called by the English Crosweeks, near the centre of the Province of New Jersey, and from eighteen to twenty miles to the south of New Brunswick. He spent the most of his time at the first and last mentioned of these places; although he made no less than four visits to the borderers on the Susquehanna, encountering dangers, privations, and sufferings of the most appalling kind; and by his last visit increasing greatly a tendency to a consumption of the lungs, which terminated his life, in about a year after his return.

Of the three fields of missionary labor, in which Mr. Brainerd was employed after his ordination, Crosweeksung was that in which he reaped, almost exclusively, the harvest of his success. On the pagans of the Susquehanna he made but little impression. Among those at the Forks of the Delaware, his interpreter, with his wife, were the only individuals who gave evidence of a sound conversion; although an external reformation of manners was visible, in a considerable number. But at Crosweeksung his success was perhaps without a parallel, in heathen missions, since the days of the apostles. For his exertions were made single-handed; he had no fellow-laborer, beyond a little occasional assistance from two or three neighboring brethren in the ministry. In opposition to discouragements which would have subdued any ordinary mind, and which went near to vanquish his own, he long persevered, with no prospect of obtaining the object of his wishes and his agonizing prayers, in the conversion of those to whom he ministered. "I do not know," he says in his journal, "that my hopes respecting the conversion of the Indians were ever reduced to so low an ebb, since I had any concern for them, as when I first visited the Indians at Crosweeksung. Yet this was the very season in which God saw fit to begin this glorious work." A glorious work it pre-eminently was. His own summary account of it is in these words:

"June 19th, 1746. This day makes up a complete year, from the first time of my preaching to these Indians in New Jersey. What amazing things has God wrought, in this space of time, for this people! What a surprising change appears in their tempers and behavior! How are morose and savage pagans, in this short period, transformed into agreeable, affectionate, and humble Christians! and their drunken and pagan howlings turned into devout and fervent praises to God! They 'who were sometimes in darkness are now become light in the Lord.' May they 'walk as children of the light and of the day!' And now, to Him that is of power to establish them, according to the Gospel and the preaching of Christ, to God only wise, be glory, through Jesus Christ, for ever and ever. Amen."

Mr. Brainerd soon became sensible, that the Gospel could not be permanently established among his Indian converts, unless he could prevail on them to abandon their wandering life as hunters, and rely for their subsistence on the cultivation of the soil. He therefore advised them—and they unanimously resolved to follow his advice—to form a compact settlement by themselves, and to become agriculturists. But for this undertaking, their residence at Crosweeksung was unfavorable, as the soil, though covered with bushes, was entirely unfit for cultivation. But the territory which they had not yet ceded to the English, was of considerable extent; and at the distance of about fifteen miles, at a place called Cranberry, they possessed a large tract of land, favorable to agricultural operations. Hither, therefore, they removed; formed a settlement without any mixture with the white population, and under the direction and instruction of their missionary, who had to take personally the charge of every concern, they entered on the business of farming. They were organized into a regular church of about forty communicating members; the whole number that removed being about one hundred and fifty. A very prosperous school of from twenty-five to thirty children, and which was eventually enlarged to fifty, was likewise established, under the instruction of an excellent master, whom Mr. Brainerd obtained for them, and for whose support he solicited donations. Some adults were also taught to read, in an evening school, opened for their accommodation. It was in this manner that Mr. Brainerd hoped he had provided for the perpetuating of Gospel ordinances, not only among the Indians already Christianized, but also for their descendants. He erected among them a house for his own residence, in the building of which a considerable part of the labor was performed by himself. This was the fourth structure, which, at his different missionary stations, he had built for the same purpose, and mostly with his own hands. Scarcely was he settled in his new abode, when his consumptive complaint compelled him to abandon both it and his beloved charge. After being confined at Elizabethtown, in the house of the Rev. Jonathan Dickinson, for about four months, he acquired strength enough to return, and bid a final farewell to his congregation of heathen converts, on the 18th of February, 1747. He died, as already stated, on the 9th of the following October, in the 30th year of his age, the half of this year not being completed. A very short time before his death, he was visited by his brother and successor, John Brainerd, and was comforted by the prospect, that in him his bereaved flock would still be under the care of a faithful, able, and affectionate pastor.

JOHN BRAINERD. The Rev. John Brainerd was a member both of the Synod and the Presbytery of New York. For several years he was successful in sustaining, and in somewhat enlarging, the Indian congregation and school, which his brother had organized. During a period in which his labors among the Indians at Cranberry were suspended, by several journeys which he made to those on the Susquehanna, and by other causes, his place was well supplied by the Rev. William Tennent, of the Presbytery of New Brunswick, whose pastoral charge was in the neighborhood of Cranberry. Mr. John Brainerd, as well as his brother, held a correspondence with the Society in Scotland for the promotion of Christian knowledge; but he was supported principally, if not wholly, by funds derived from the contributions of Presbyterian congregations in America. Such was certainly the fact, after the commencement of our Revolutionary war. The Synod had previously allowed him a salary of thirty pounds per annum; and in 1763 they ordered a collection to be taken up in all their congregations, for the support of the Indian Mission. To the schoolmaster they awarded, for that year, an allowance of thirty pounds. They also voted sixty-five pounds, for the support of the Rev. Sampson Occum, a native Indian, a member of the Presbytery of Suffolk, on Long Island, and at that time a missionary among the Oneida Indians. He was afterwards employed, for many years, among various tribes of his race.

The converts from paganism who were gathered into the Christian Church by the Brainerds, appear to have maintained, with very few exceptions, a character for vital piety and exemplary deportment, through the whole of their subsequent life; and some are represented as having died in the triumphant hope of the Gospel. But from a variety of causes which cannot now be specified, but chiefly from being deprived of their lands by the fraud and cupidity of the white inhabitants, their numbers were greatly reduced.* In 1802, some commissioners from New Jersey conducted eighty-five Delaware Indians, the remainder of Mr. John Brainerd's congregation, to New Stockbridge, to place them under the ministry of Mr. Sergeant, the missionary in that town; and it was then stated that after Mr. Brainerd's death (in 1780) they were left alone, having no spiritual shepherd to watch over them, no meetings for divine worship on the Sabbath, and no school for their children. We only add that the remnant left, seem to have lost all sense of religion; and it is believed have now become nearly, if not altogether, extinct—the common fate of Indians when surrounded by a white population.

In the year 1766, the Rev. Charles Beatty and the Rev. George Duffield, performed a mission, by the appointment of the Synod, among the Indians on the Muskingum River, in what is now the State of Ohio, but which was then a howling wilderness. An account of this mission was published in a printed pamphlet; and the representation made was so favorable, that in the

* Brown's History of Missions, vol. i., p. 136.

following year the Synod appointed two other missionaries to the same region; but owing to unfavorable reports of the state of things among the Indians and the
frontier inhabitants, this mission was not fulfilled; and
no further attempts were made to evangelize the heathen
in that quarter.

THE NEW YORK SOCIETY. In 1796, the New York Missionary Society was organized, consisting principally of members of the Presbyterian Church. It owed
its origin to the missionary zeal excited by the accounts
then recently received in this country, of the institution, animated exertions, and flattering prospects of
the London Missionary Society. The present writer
can state from a distinct recollection of his feelings and
language at the period now referred to, that although he
highly approved the zeal of the founders of this Society,
and was perfectly willing that they should prosecute
their own views of duty, yet for himself he saw no need
of any new organization for missionary operations in
the Presbyterian Church. He thought the zeal now
awakened should be cherished, and be carried into the
General Assembly of our Church; that in this body we
already had an organization, than which none could be
devised better adapted to the prosecution of foreign as
well as domestic missions; in a word, it was his opinion
that every member of the Presbyterian Church should
use his influence, and all his means, for evangelizing the
heathen, through the agency of the Supreme Judicatory
of our Church. How far these sentiments prevailed is
not known; but it was only in the northern section of
the Presbyterian Church, that societies, similar to that
now under consideration, were at that time patronized.
The members of this Society, however, though not very
numerous, proceeded with a laudable spirit and activity

in the execution of their plans. They collected funds to a considerable amount; and under their patronage one of their missionaries, with his son as a schoolmaster, formed a missionary establishment among the Chickasaw Indians, which for a time prospered, and promised to be permanent. No less than eighteen individuals went out with this mission, and contributed in various ways to carry its design into effect. The Society also established two Indian missions in the State of New York; one in the Tuscarora, and the other in the Seneca tribe. Both these missions, especially the latter, appear to have prospered; and to have been happily instrumental in gathering a number of the heathen, as hopeful converts, into the Christian Church. In the year 1821, they transferred all their missions to the United Foreign Missionary Society.

THE NORTHERN SOCIETY. In 1797, the Northern Missionary Society was instituted. Why a distinct society was so soon formed in the neighborhood of that last mentioned, and what was the proportion of members of the Presbyterian Church which it embodied, is unknown to the present writer. Commendable exertions, however, were made by this institution, to promote Indian missions. The Society obtained considerable funds, and the Indians themselves made it a valuable donation of land. In the circular letter sent in 1802, by the Standing Committee of Missions, to the missionary establishments of Europe, it is stated that this Society had then "made preparations for sending a minister of the Gospel and a schoolmaster, to the Oneida nation of Indians." It also appears that it had a mission located at Fort Gratiot, which was assumed by the United Foreign Missionary Society in 1823, and transferred to the American Board in 1826; at which time, it employed one male and two female teachers, and had established a school, containing from fifteen to twenty Indian children.

In the appointment of Mr. Chapman, as a missionary to the northwestern frontier of the State of New York, in the year 1800, the General Assembly had a reference, not only to the wants of the white population, but to the deplorable condition of the Indian tribes, for whom their sympathy was deeply enlisted. Hence, in the circular letter addressed to the Presbyteries by the Standing Committee, in 1802, the following passage appeared: "Missionaries for the Indians is a great desideratum with the Assembly. The hope of contributing to send the Gospel to the heathen tribes, prompted the liberality of many who have contributed most largely to the funds which the Assembly have at command; and it was with the deepest regret that the last Assembly found that they had not a single candidate for an Indian mission. If your Presbytery can nominate one who is well qualified, it will be an important acquisition."

The next year (1803) the desideratum of the Assembly was obtained. The Rev. Gideon Blackburn was found willing to engage in a mission to the Cherokee Indians.

MISSION TO THE CHEROKEE INDIANS. Mr. Blackburn was accordingly recommended by the Committee, and appointed by the Assembly. With great zeal, activity, and devotedness, he prosecuted his missionary undertaking for eight years. But the failure of his health (in 1810), and a necessary removal of his family to a greater distance from the field of missionary labor, compelled him to retire, when he seemed to be on the point of reaping the fruits of his toils and sufferings. This was a subject of great regret to the Committee, to the Assembly, and to many others, who had taken a lively interest in this promising mission.

Mr. Blackburn's efforts were principally directed to the establishment of schools among the Cherokees. By these schools he hoped to promote their civilization, to prepare them for an advantageous hearing of the Gospel in public preaching, and for a permanent enjoyment of its ordinances. He also had it in view to qualify the Indian youth, not only for the duties of secular life, but for ministerial usefulness, when, by the blessing of God, any of them should become practically pious. Two flourishing schools were established ; for the support of one of which, he made himself personally and exclusively responsible. For sustaining the other, the annual allowance made by the Assembly, for several years, was five hundred dollars; and to this, in one year, an addition of three hundred dollars was made by the New Jersey Missionary Society. Not less than ten thousand dollars were expended on this mission; more than half of which was obtained by Mr. Blackburn himself, in donations and contributions which he received, chiefly, in a journey which he made for the purpose through the New England States. The amount of his receipts, as stated by himself, was five thousand three hundred and forty-seven dollars and ninety cents.

The ability, assiduity, and fidelity of Mr. Blackburn in his missionary employment, not only among the Indians, but in preaching the Gospel to the white population in the vicinity of the Cherokee country, was attested by the Governor of the State of Tennessee, by other respectable individuals, and by the Presbytery of Union. The rapid improvement of the youth in his Indian schools was truly surprising. The specimens of their handwriting, and of some articles of their manufacture, which were transmitted to the Committee, manifested a progress in improvement of the most promising kind. In 1806, there were in the two schools seventy-five scholars, whose proficiency in reading, writing, and arithmetic exceeded the most sanguine expectations which had previously been entertained. But the improvement of the Cherokees, during the mission of Mr. Blackburn, was not confined to the schools. The Indians in general, made no inconsiderable progress in many of the common and most useful arts of life. They assumed, to a great extent, not only the habits, but even the form of government, of a civilized nation. At a kind of national meeting, they formed a constitution, chose a legislative body, and passed a number of laws, among which was an act imposing taxes for public purposes.

In a letter from Mr. Blackburn, of January 5, 1810, the following interesting statement of the progress of the Cherokee Indians, towards a state of civilization, was contained: "In the nation there are twelve thousand three hundred and ninety-five Indians. The number of females exceeds that of the males, by two hundred. The whites in the nation are three hundred and forty-one. Of these, there are one hundred and thirteen who have Indian wives. Of negro slaves there are five hundred and eighty-three. The number of their cattle is nineteen thousand five hundred; of their horses six thousand one hundred; of their hogs nineteen thousand six hundred; of their sheep one thousand and thirty-seven. They have now in actual operation thirteen grist mills, three saw mills, three saltpetre works, and one powder mill. They have fifty wagons; between four hundred and eighty and five hundred ploughs; one thousand six hundred spinning wheels; four hundred and sixty-seven looms, and forty-nine silversmiths.

"Circulating specie is supposed to be as plenty among them as is common among the white people. Most of these advantages they have acquired since the year 1796, and particularly since 1803." There is a more extended detail, accompanied by calculations, which we have not room to insert; but it may be seen, in the appendix to Brown's 1st volume of the History of Missions, page 505.

It was the intention of the Standing Committee of Missions of the Assembly, to prosecute the Cherokee Mission; but while they were looking for missionaries possessing suitable qualifications for the work, the Rev. Mr. Kingsbury, acting under the authority of the American Board of Commissioners for Foreign Missions, passed through Philadelphia, to occupy the field in which the missionaries of the General Assembly had been laboring for eight years. When Mr. Kingsbury waited on the Chairman of the Standing Committee, to know if there was any objection to his mission to the Cherokees, he was informed that the Committee could not object to his laboring for the benefit of that benighted people; but at the same time, he was distinctly apprised of their design to resume the mission, so soon as Providence should be pleased to furnish them with suitable missionaries. The subsequent success of the missionaries of the American Board, in this "line of things made ready to their hand," was most happy; and rendered unnecessary any farther efforts of the Standing Committee to prosecute a mission in the Cherokee country.

MISSION AMONG THE WYANDOT INDIANS. In 1805, the Standing Committee of the General Assembly received a letter (dated October 23 of that year) from the Secretary of "The Board of Trust of the Western

Missionary Society," composed of members, and acting under the direction, of the Synod of Pittsburgh, and chartered by the State of Pennsylvania, requesting pecuniary aid in establishing a mission among the Wyandot Indians. The Committee could not act officially in answer to the request of the Board of Trust, till authorized so to do by the General Assembly; but one of their members immediately made them a donation of one hundred dollars, and the Assembly of the following year appropriated four hundred dollars to their funds. The same sum was awarded to them annually, for several years in succession. Sandusky, in the State of Ohio, was selected by the Board, for the location of their missionary establishment. Their ultimate design was to evangelize the savages; but to facilitate the attainment of this great object, they organized a school for the instruction of their children, whom they both fed and clothed. They also procured land, for the purpose of assisting, by its cultivation, in the support of the establishment; as well as to instruct and engage the Indians in the business of farming. On the farm, they erected the necessary buildings, and the school consisted of from thirty to forty pupils. This mission was going on in a very prosperous way, till the war of 1812; when the buildings having been burned, and the improvements destroyed by the enemy, the mission was suspended. An effort was made to revive it after the war, but with little success.

MISSION AT CORNPLANTER'S TOWN. In 1814 the Western Board, in consequence of a personal and pressing application from Cornplanter, a distinguished chief of the Six Nations, resolved to establish a mission among his people. The Indians, who had requested this mission, received very cordially the missionary and schoolmaster who were sent to them, engaged to provide for their own children boarding and lodging, without any expense to the Society; and the chief promised to furnish a school-house and a dwelling for the teacher, together with a farm, if it should be judged necessary to promote the design of the mission. This chief seemed to have a deep sense of the importance of the Christian religion, both for himself and his people; and to be exceedingly desirous that they should learn and practice the arts and usages of civilized life. The General Assembly agreed to allow three hundred dollars toward the support of this mission. But the instruction of these Indians was, after a short time, assumed by another denomination of Christians; and in the autumn of 1818, the school at Cornplanter's town, owing to the occurrence of several obstacles, and the removal of a number of the Indian families from the town and the adjacent country, was discontinued. The Board of Trust, reluctant to lose altogether the fruits of their labor and liberality, endeavored to persuade a number of the Indian boys, who had made some considerable progress, to prosecute their education; and offered, as an encouragement, to bring them into Christian society, and to clothe, support, and instruct them gratuitously. This benevolent offer, however, was not accepted, and the Board were compelled, at least for a time, to resign their hopes of further success.

[The Cornplanter station is again, in 1891, under the care of the Presbyterian Church, in connection with the mission to the Seneca Indians. Brief but interesting accounts of its condition are given in the recent Annual Reports of the Board. The band consists now of about a hundred souls, and most of the adults are members of the Church. Under the Board of Trust their settlement was visited, to preach the Gospel to them by such pastors as Messrs. McPherrin and Tait, and several years were spent in their service by lay missionaries.]

MISSION AT LEWISTOWN, OHIO. In 1814, a mission at Lewistown in Ohio was projected, for the benefit of the Indians in that vicinity. In the following year, four hundred and fifty dollars were granted to the Rev. James Hughes, who was about to remove to Ohio, and offered to undertake the mission. Here, as elsewhere, the prospect of benefiting the benighted pagans seemed to be highly promising, and yet it ended in disappointment. It is deserving of notice, that however unproductive of other beneficial results, were the Indian Missions undertaken and patronized by the General Assembly, they seem to have had a happy effect in preventing savage barbarities, on the frontiers of our country. It appears that not one of the tribes that the Assembly attempted to evangelize, took any hostile part in the existing conflict, during the war of 1812.

In 1816, the General Assembly adopted measures which resulted next year in the establishment of the United Foreign Missionary Society.

UNITED FOREIGN SOCIETY. Believing that a new Society for conducting Foreign Missions might be advantageously formed, the Assembly of that year entered into a correspondence on the subject, with the Reformed Dutch Church, and the Associated Reformed Church. The proposition made, met with a cordial reception from the supreme judicatories of these sister Churches; and the Committee which had been appointed to manage the concern on the part of the Assembly, reported, at the next meeting of that body, the Constitution which had been prepared for the contemplated Society; and which, after some amendments, adopted in the following year, stood as expressed in the following articles:

"1. The Society shall be composed of the Presbyterian, Reformed Dutch, and Associate Reformed Churches, and all others who may choose to join them; and shall be known by the name of The United Foreign Missionary Society.

"2. The object of the Society shall be, to spread the Gospel among the Indians of North America, the inhabitants of Mexico, and South America, and other portions of the heathen and anti-Christian world.

"3. The business of the Society shall be conducted by a Board, consisting of a President, six Vice-Presidents, a Corresponding Secretary, a Recording Secretary, a Treasurer, and eighteen Managers, to be annually chosen by the Society. They shall have power to enact their own by-laws. Seven shall constitute a quorum.

"4. The Board shall present their annual report to the highest judicatory of the three denominations, for their information.

"5. Any person paying three dollars annually, or thirty dollars at one time, shall be a member of the Society; and any person presenting to the Society a donation of not less than one hundred dollars, shall be a director for life, and entitled to a seat and vote in the Board of Managers.

"6. The President, Treasurer, and Secretary of any Society auxiliary to this, shall be ex officio members of the Board of Managers.

"7. The Board of Managers shall be authorized to fill any vacancies that may occur in the Board.

"8. The annual meeting of the Society shall be in the city of New York on the ——— .

"9. Missionaries shall be selected from the three Churches indiscriminately.

"10. This Constitution may be altered by a vote of two-thirds of the members present at an annual meeting, with the consent of the highest judicatory of the three denominations."

The operations of this Society were commenced with vigor and unanimity, and with prospects apparently the most auspicious. The United States Government, then under the presidency of Mr. Monroe, gave it countenance and patronage—allotting to its establishments a liberal portion of the fund annually appropriated by Congress to the civilization of the Indians. The Superintendent of Indian Trade, Col. Thomas L. McKenney, could scarcely have embarked in its favor with more zeal and activity, if the whole concern had been his own. The supreme judicatories of the united denominations, made earnest and repeated appeals to the Churches under their supervision—urging them to liberal contributions to support the establishments which they were pledged to sustain, and to earnest, united, and constant prayer for their success. Numerous auxiliary Societies and Associations were formed, to aid the operations of the general Board; and toward the close of its existence, subordinate Boards of Agency were established at Pittsburgh, Cincinnati, Louisville in Kentucky, and St. Louis in Missouri. An interesting monthly publication, entitled *The American Missionary Register*, was issued, containing particular information of the state, progress, prospects, and necessities of the several Missions under the direction of the Board, and a general survey of other missions, both domestic and foreign, with biographical notices of eminent deceased missionaries. The appointed officers and agents of the Society were active and laborious, as well as intelligent, in the discharge of their duties severally; and the missionaries they employed were in general competent, as well as faithful, devoted, and persevering—not disheartened by the sickness which often prevailed, and the deaths which not unfrequently occurred among them.

No extended detail of the proceedings of the Board, or of the results of its plans and efforts, can be given in this compendious view. The writer is indebted to the kindness of the Secretary for domestic correspondence, Mr. Z. Lewis, for a summary statement of the missions established, and of some other important particulars, of which he will avail himself; and to which he will subjoin a few additional remarks. Mr. Lewis states, that "The United Foreign Missionary Society established in 1820, the Union Mission, among the Osages of the Arkansas; in 1821, the Harmony Mission, among the Osages of the Missouri; in 1822, the Cattaraugus Mission, in Western New York; in 1823, the Mackinaw Mission, in Michigan Territory; in 1824, the Haytian Mission, in the Island of Hayti; in all, five missions. Four other missions were transferred to us, as follows: in 1821, the Tuscarora and Seneca Missions, by the New York Missionary Society; in 1823, the Fort Gratiot Mission, in Michigan, by the Northern Missionary Society; and in 1825, the Maumee Mission, on the Maumee River, by the Western Missionary Society at Pittsburgh. Thus when our missionary interests were transferred to the American Board of Commissioners for Foreign Missions, we had under our care nine Missions, embracing sixty male and female missionaries; two hundred and fifty children and youth, including six beneficiaries at the Foreign Mission School in Connecticut; and more than forty native converts to the faith and hope of the Gospel."

THE TWO OSAGE MISSIONS. In a brief review of the missions thus mentioned by Mr. Lewis, it is painful to remark, that the two Osage Missions, although the first established, and always the most expensive, yet were those in which there was the least success. Till about the middle of August, 1823, when, by the interposition and influence of the agents of the general government, peace was established among the Osages and the Cherokees, there had been, between those tribes, from the time of the arrival of the missionaries in the Osage country, a state of ceaseless hostility. From this cause, the mission families were often placed in very perilous circumstances; and though, under the protection of a kind Providence, they eventually escaped personal violence, and sustained no material loss of property, yet their plans and efforts for the benefit of the benighted pagans were all marred and constantly held in check. Beside the erection of mills, the enclosure and cultivation of large fields, and the establishment of a smithery, schools were opened, and the Indians were invited and urged to send their children for instruction. But a general and standing excuse for keeping them from school was, the danger to which they would be exposed from their enemies, if absent from their parents. That this excuse was little else than a pretence, was proved by the slow and small increase of the schools, after the restoration of peace. In August, 1823, there were in the school at Harmony, but eighteen children, thirteen girls and five boys; and at the Union school, the whole number was only thirteen. In 1825, the school at Harmony had reached its maximum number of thirty-six pupils; and at Union the number varied from fourteen to twenty; and in the few instances in which some serious impressions of religion seemed to be made, the hopes of the missionaries were ultimately disappointed.

If there was ever a single Osage who became a Christian convert, and held fast his integrity, it is unknown to the author of this sketch; so that the native converts mentioned by Mr. Lewis, must have been among the heathen of the other missionary stations. At those located in western New York, it is known that promising Christian churches were established; a considerable number of hopeful converts were also made at other missionary stations, whose members were mostly native Indians.

Since the above was written, the writer has seen with pleasure, in the *Missionary Herald* for March, 1838, the following statement from a missionary to the Cherokees of Arkansas: "The Osage young woman, who has been brought up by the mission, aids in the management of the girls out of school. She has been a professor of religion for several years, and seems to be a true follower of Christ."

The want of success among the Osages does not appear to have been attributable to any defect of fidelity, zeal, or diligence in the missionaries employed by the United Foreign Missionary Society; and whatever appearances of a change for the better, if such there were, under the management of the American Board, those appearances must have been temporary and evanescent. The *Missionary Herald* for the month of January, of the present year, contains the following melancholy statement: "Mr. Requa, the only remaining individual of the Osage mission, and who had himself nearly determined to abandon his work there in discouragement, visited their towns last autumn. It seemed to him that the providence of God was clearly calling to a re-establishment of the mission, and accordingly, after corresponding with the Committee, he examined their reservation, and selected a favorable spot for a large agricultural colony, and made considerable progress in preparing the requisite buildings and other improvements. A preacher and schoolmaster were expected to join him, as soon as circumstances would permit. But during the past summer, the hostility of other portions of the tribe to the new establishment, and apparently to all measures for introducing Christian knowledge and the arts of civilized life among them, became manifest. So great was the annoyance suffered, and so little prospect of usefulness, or even of safety to the settlers and the mission property, did there seem to be, that in the month of July, Mr. Requa removed his effects, and left the reservation. No mission station is maintained among the Osages."

The last accounts from the Osage tribe, represent this unhappy people as in the most deplorable state of misery and destitution—suffering and dying of absolute famine.

THE CATTARAUGUS MISSION. The Cattaraugus Mission was located near the shores of Lake Erie, about thirty miles from Buffalo. The Indians of this station were only a section of the Seneca tribe; and both the Senecas and Tuscaroras were greatly divided on the subject of receiving Christian missionaries, the Christian party being earnestly in favor of their reception, and the more numerous pagan party decisively opposed to their instructions, and even to their residing on the Indian reservations. The principal chief of the Seneca nation, known by the name of Red Jacket, was avowedly and till the day of his death, which but recently occurred, determinately and inveterately hostile, both to civilization and the Christian religion. The United Foreign Missionary Society, however, were fortunate enough to secure the services of a teacher, who, under their patronage, established the most prosperous school at this station which they ever founded. The managers, in their eighth report, the last before the transfer to the American Board, speaking of the Cattaraugus Mission, make the following statement: "The continued progress of this Mission is highly gratifying to your Managers. The school, at our last anniversary, embraced forty-five children, twenty-five having since been added, the present number is seventy. By their general deportment, by the proficiency they have made in learning to read and write, and the cheerfulness and skill with which they have performed the duties assigned to them out of school, the children have gained the commendation and esteem of their instructors. Some of the older boys have manifested a more than ordinary seriousness of character. Impressed with a sense of their danger as sinners, they have been discovered in little weeping circles, renouncing the pagan's hope, and uniting their hearts in prayer to the Christian's God and Saviour. Several of the chiefs, in the view of your Superintendent, give evidence of piety. They are anxiously looking forward to the appointment of a minister of the Gospel for that station; and are only waiting the organization of a missionary church, to make a public and formal renunciation of the pagan standard, and to enroll their names under the banner of the cross."

THE MACKINAW MISSION. The Mackinaw Mission, on the island of Michilimacinach, in the strait or broad stream which connects Lake Huron with Lake Michigan, was supposed to occupy a position peculiarly favorable to extensive missionary operations. In the report of the Managers, referred to in the foregoing article, they say: "In the opinion of the Superintendent [of this mission] the field of missionary labor at this station, may be just as wide as the most extended charities and active exertions of the Church please to make it." This opinion is confirmed by a letter from a respectable officer of the garrison at Sault de St. Marie, and by the verbal communications of a judicious and intelligent citizen of that place. They all concur in the opinion, that Mackinaw, in point of local situation, is better calculated for a missionary establishment, than any other part of that western region; and that, to future missionaries, it will prove the key of entrance into a number of distant and populous tribes."

The Rev. William M. Ferry, who had previously resided at Mackinaw for about ten months, and who tendered his services to the Board, was appointed superintendent of the Mission. A letter of instructions was sent to his residence at Northampton, in Massachusetts, and he speedily repaired, with his wife, to the place of his destination. A promising school was opened, which at the time the mission was transferred, in its infant state, to the American Board, contained nearly fifty Indian children. A female teacher, in addition to Mrs. Ferry, was employed in this school.

THE HAYTIAN MISSION. The Haytian Mission was intended for the benefit of the colored people of the United States, who, influenced by the favorable prospects presented to them in Hayti, by the constituted authorities of that island, resorted thither in great numbers, in 1824. The United Foreign Missionary Society appointed two missionaries of the colored race, Mr. Pennington, of New York, and Mr. Hughes, of Philadelphia, both ordained ministers, to visit Hayti; to preach to the emigrants, and when circumstances should favor, to form one or more Presbyterian churches among them. They repaired to the field of their missionary labor; but soon left it, without effecting anything valuable, although they were kindly received. A ruling elder of the First African Presbyterian Church of Philadelphia has stated to the writer, since this sketch has been in preparation, that he was in Hayti when the missionaries arrived; that he became acquainted with them; that such were the discouraging circumstances in which they found the emigrants, that they scarcely attempted to preach; that they stayed on the Island not more than three months, and then returned to this country; as did many others who were disappointed like themselves.

THE TUSCARORA MISSION. The Tuscarora Mission, located about four miles east of Lewistown, Niagara County, New York, had been under the care of the New York Missionary Society about twenty years, when it was transferred to the United Foreign Missionary Society in 1821. At the time of the transfer, the establishment possessed a missionary farm of about a hundred and forty acres, with a good house, barn, and orchard; about forty acres of the farm were enclosed, and under the cultivation of an experienced farmer, with his family. There was at the station, one missionary, the Rev. James C. Crane; a regularly organized church, comprising seventeen Indian members; and preparations had been made to erect a new council-house, and also a church edifice of larger dimensions and more convenient structure, than that which had hitherto been occupied. The Indians generally lived in comfortable dwellings, and had made no inconsiderable progress in civilization, possessed a good deal of property, all the implements of husbandry, and some of their youth had made good proficiency in the elementary parts of an English education. This mission was somewhat improved, during the five years it was under the care of the United Society, but the details cannot be inserted in this limited sketch. The result may be judged of by a single extract from the journal of its Superintendent, the Rev. Thomas Harris, written three months after it had been made over to the American Board. The extract relates to a sacramental season, and is as follows:

"August 29, 1826. Went to the Tuscarora village on Saturday, and met with the Church and congregation on the Sabbath. The assembly, though small, appeared to be devout. To me it was a privilege truly delightful, to hold out to the scattered of Christ's flock on this thirsty hill, the symbols of a Saviour's death; and to witness with what tears of joy and thankfulness many came forward, and received the tokens of his love.

"There has been at this station, for a few months past, a more than usual seriousness among some of the young people. Six or seven persons have appeared for some time, to be anxiously inquiring the way to heaven. I requested all the inquirers to meet me on Monday afternoon. I was deeply affected with the indications of the Divine Spirit with us. Such appeared to be the tenderness of conscience, the deep and powerful conviction of the hatefulness of sin, and the earnestness of desire to be delivered from its power, that I could not for a moment doubt, that God had been among them by his Spirit; and in the case of three or four 'wounded mightily.' Some of these persons were so affected in conversing with me, that they sobbed and cried aloud for some time. They say that frequently they have such an awful sense of their past iniquity, that they cannot help crying out."

FOREIGN OR HEATHEN MISSIONS.

THE SENECA MISSION. The Seneca Mission was located four or five miles from Buffalo, near the outlet of Lake Erie, and was commenced by the New York Missionary Society in 1811, and transferred to the United Foreign Missionary Society, along with the Tuscarora Mission, in 1821. When assumed by the latter Society, the property of this mission consisted of two dwelling-houses and a school-house, together with the use, for an indefinite period, of the ground on which they were erected. This tribe, doubtless under the influence of Red Jacket, their principal chief, had refused to permit a preacher of the Gospel to reside among them; although they allowed a school to be opened for the instruction of their children; and the teacher of this school, with his wife, were the only missionaries at this station, when it was relinquished by the New York Missionary Society. Immediately afterwards, however, two additional female teachers were appointed for the school; and the Christian party now requested the United Foreign Missionary Society to send them a minister of the Gospel, who might reside in the near neighborhood, but not within the bounds of the Indian reservation. This request, after some time, was granted, and public worship was performed in the mission house of the establishment. In April, 1823, a missionary church was organized, consisting of four men, three of whom were chiefs; and on this occasion, the congregation assembled in the council-house.

The Legislature of New York rejected a petition presented to them, praying that ministers of the Gospel might be permitted to reside on the Indian lands; and at one time the civil authorities of that State entirely disbanded and broke up the Seneca Mission. The Indians petitioned the Legislature for redress, and their application was, in the first instance, refused; but a second application, in which a large number of their chiefs and warriors joined, was successful, and the mission was resumed. The school which was established at this station, was of a most promising character, and when transferred to the American Board, consisted of forty-three pupils; but it is believed that no more of the native Indians than the four individuals already mentioned, belonged to the mission church at that time.

[The Seneca, Tuscarora, and Tonawanda Missions, in Western New York, after their connection with the American Board until 1870, with an encouraging record, were then transferred to the Board of Foreign Missions of the Presbyterian Church. They are still under its care, and are reported as in a prospering condition.—See Annual Report, 1892, pages 151–153. The number of communicants in six churches is 372, of whom 47 were received last year.]

THE FORT GRATIOT MISSION. The Fort Gratiot Mission, in the Michigan Territory, was located on the river St. Clair, about one mile below the outlet of Lake Huron; and when transferred by the Northern Missionary Society, it consisted of one male and two female teachers, and an Indian school of from fifteen to twenty children.

The author of this sketch has not been able to obtain any information relative to the changes which may have taken place, for the better or the worse, in this mission, during the time, about two years and a half, that it was under the superintendence of the United Foreign Missionary Society.

THE MAUMEE MISSION. The Maumee Mission, organized in 1822, by the Board of Trust of the Synod of Pittsburgh, and transferred to the United Foreign Missionary Society in 1825, was located on the Maumee River, near Fort Meigs, in Wood County, and State of Ohio. This mission was under the superintendence of the Society to which it was transferred, but about seven months; and probably underwent no changes whatever during that period. In giving a compendious view of it, therefore, the writer will avail himself of communications received from the Rev. E. P. Swift, the Secretary of the Board of Trust, relative to the origin of the mission, and to its general state and operations, while connected with that Board. The substance of Mr. Swift's statement is as follows:

"The Board of Trust of the Synod of Pittsburgh, after various incipient measures, resolved, at a meeting held in Pittsburgh, February 6, 1822, to institute, in the coming summer, a mission among the Ottaway Indians, on the banks of the Maumee River. At a subsequent meeting, the Rev. Elisha McCurdy was appointed to repair to the Land-office in Ohio, and enter for the Board, from one to two hundred acres of land, adjoining the Indian reservation; and from thence proceed to the site of the contemplated mission, and superintend the erection of suitable buildings for their accommodation. After the close of the Synod in the fall, the Board having, during the preceding summer, conferred with and appointed various persons for the intended service, met in the city of Pittsburgh, and with appropriate religious exercises, constituted a mission family, to go to the said Ottaway tribe of Indians. The family consisted of twenty-one individuals; two of them ministers of the Gospel, and two others, teachers for a school intended to be opened; the others, many of whom were females, were to be employed as assistants to the family, the school and the farm. The Rev. Samuel Tait was appointed, pro tempore, the Superintendent of the mission. After having thus been set apart to their work, the missionary family repaired to their field of labor. A promising school was shortly afterwards opened; stated meetings were commenced—the missionaries preaching through an interpreter—and improvements on the land purchased were undertaken. The Rev. Mr. Tait, having fulfilled his temporary appointment, returned to his people in the spring; and in September following, (1823), the Rev. Ludovicus Robbins, then of the Presbytery of Washington, Pennsylvania, having been appointed to succeed Mr. Tait, in July preceding, was publicly set apart as Superintendent of the mission, and joined his brethren at the station shortly afterwards. One of the preachers and one other individual, did not continue long in connection with the mission; but their places were supplied by a physician (who was also to act as schoolmaster), his wife, and another female missionary. Up to the autumn of 1825, at which time the station, on application of the United Foreign Missionary Society, was transferred to that Board, was well sustained—chiefly by the churches within the bounds of the Synod of Pittsburgh; although the Board were, for the whole period, considerably engaged in appointing and sustaining missionaries in feeble churches, and in new and destitute settlements.

"As to the results of the Mission, I could not easily give you particulars; and besides, you will perceive from the date of the transfer, that the station did not continue under our care long after its operations were fairly commenced. We had a promising school at the station, for the most of the time; and as far as I can recollect, two or three of its pupils became hopefully pious. Through the instrumentality of the missionaries, much good was done to one or two infant churches in the white settlements, in the vicinity, which were supplied with the means of grace by them. In the year 1823, the Board appointed the Rev. Robert M. Laird, pastor of the church at Princess Ann, Maryland, as an exploring agent, to visit the region of the Upper Lakes, to labor at the Military station at the Sault de St. Marie, Michigan Territory, and to hold consultations with the various tribes of Indians in that region, on the subject of missionary schools, and in general to collect information from various quarters, on all points connected with the tribes, character, number, and wants of the Aborigines of the United States. Mr. Laird spent about nine months in that service, principally laboring at the Military post, and in the garrison. A considerable revival of religion took place among the officers and soldiers, under his ministry, and numbers gave credible evidence of a change of heart. The Board contemplated the establishment of a mission in the region of Lake Superior; but the proposal and prospect of the transfer of their operations to New York, led them to defer any further measures at the time."

The *Missionary Herald* for the month of April, 1826, furnishes, from a report to which Mr. Swift refers, some important information relative to the Indian school at Maumee. A part of it is as follows:

"The number of scholars in the school is thirty-one, of whom seventeen are boys. Six of the pupils are from the Chippeway tribe, nine are Wyandots, three Potawatomies, four Ottawas, four Miamies, four Shawnees, and one Munsee. Their ages are from seven to twenty-two; one, however, is twenty-seven. Twenty can read the Bible, thirteen write, five are studying arithmetic, four geography, and three grammar." A part of a letter is then given from Mr. Van Tassel, the teacher of the school, of which the following are extracts: "Before I came here, I had taught school several years, and I can assure you, sir, that these scholars excel in writing any white children I ever taught. In short, the children are all making such progress in their studies as affords a high degree of satisfaction to their instructors, and we presume that could our patrons and Christian friends witness their docility, their submission to authority, and the eagerness with which they listen to instruction drawn from the Bible, they would not feel as if they were laboring in vain, or spending their money for naught. For a few weeks past, the scholars have been exercising their talents in writing composition, and they frequently hand billets to their teacher and other members of the family." Copies of three of these billets are then given, after which the teacher adds: "Many more equally good have been handed in, but these will be sufficient to give a specimen of their improvement, and show you the state of their minds. They all appear united, cheerful, and happy—as much or more so than could reasonably be expected, while they are destitute of the benign religion of Jesus. O if they could all enjoy this, we should have a little paradise here below. For this we pray, and for this we beg a special interest in your prayers to Almighty God, with whom is the residue of the Spirit."

Having completed a survey of the missions instituted by the United Foreign Missionary Society, and of those received under its care, it may now be proper to inquire what were the causes which had influence in producing the transfer of all its concerns to the American Board of Commissioners for Foreign Missions, and the consequent dissolution of the Society itself. A heavy debt, contracted by the Society, and which it knew not how to meet, was the principal cause publicly assigned for this transfer, at the time it was made. That this was one cause is not questioned; but that it was not the only, or even the chief cause, is manifest from the published transactions which took place, between the party which made and that which accepted the transfer. The following query was proposed to Mr. Lewis: "Was the want of funds the chief inducement?" In reply, he says: "So far as I know this was the only inducement. In May, 1825, having served the Board faithfully and gratuitously for five years, as their principal Secretary, and finding that my health began to yield under my heavy labors, and having the satisfaction of seeing the Society, for the first time, free from debt; I resigned my office, in favor of Mr. Crane, and removed my family to the country for the summer. On my return to the city in September, I found, to my astonishment, that the drafts upon the Board, and other expenses, had, in four months, exceeded the receipts, by nearly ten thousand dollars; that the Board, as well as the Treasurer, had become alarmed; that they had determined to offer the whole concern to the Eastern Board, on condition that it would assume our debt; and that Commissioners had gone to lay the proposition before the Board, then in session." Mr. Lewis afterwards says: "I do not assert that the want of funds was the only inducement [to the transfer], but that it was the only one mentioned to me." He then tells the querist that for further information, if desired, recourse must be had to two gentlemen, "who," he says, "I understood were the leading actors in the project of the transfer." These gentlemen have not been consulted; for if the Society was out of debt entirely, but four months before the transfer; and if the amount of debt, at the time it took place, did not exceed ten thousand dollars; and if, as we know was the fact, three respectable religious denominations were morally bound and even solemnly pledged, to see this debt discharged, it cannot be credited that there were not other, and more powerful, motives prompting to the transfer, than the fact that the United Foreign Missionary Society owed ten thousand dollars. The avowed and undoubtedly the real reasons, which operated in this concern, are distinctly set forth in the published proceedings of the American Board, at their annual meeting in September, 1825, and inserted in the October number of the *Missionary Herald* of the same year. They are as follows:

"In the first two days, the subject of amalgamating the [United] Foreign Missionary Society with the Board came several times under consideration. A committee, appointed to confer with the Commissioners from that Society, reported, that so far as they had been able to examine the subject, the proposed union is both practicable and desirable. The Commissioners then made statements to the Board, similar to those which they had previously made to the Committee. The reasons which they adduced in favor of a union with the Board were briefly these:

"That the most friendly relations and feelings now exist between the General Assembly and the Synods, and the Orthodox Association of New England:

"That the spirit of controversy having subsided, the intelligent and candid of the Christian public are all satisfied, that the same Gospel which is preached in the Middle and Southern and Western States, is preached also in the Eastern States:

"That the missionaries of both Societies preach precisely the same Gospel to the heathen; and that the same regulations are adopted by both, in the management of missions:

"That both derive much of their funds from the same churches and individuals; that the great body of Christians do not perceive or make any distinction between the two institutions; and consequently do not perceive any necessity for two, and regret the existence of two; and that many churches and individuals, unwilling to evince a preference for either, are thus prevented from acting promptly, and contributing liberally to either:

"That both Societies are evidently embarrassed, and cramped, through the fear of collision and difficulty; and that the agents of both are discouraged, and limited in their operations, by the same apprehension:

"That the objects, principles, and operations of both are so entirely similar, that there can be no good reason assigned for maintaining two:

"That the claims upon the churches are becoming so numerous, and frequent, and the necessities of the destitute so urgent, that all institutions are sacredly bound to observe the most rigid economy; and that by the union, much that is now expended for the support of offices, officers, agents, etc., will be saved for the general objects of the Societies:

"And lastly, that the prevailing feeling in the churches demands a union between the two Societies, and will eventually make it unavoidably necessary:

"After these statements, a committee was appointed to report the terms on which they supposed the union might be formed with the United Foreign Missionary Society. Their report, after much and deliberate discussion, was unanimously adopted by the Board, and received the concurrence of the Commissioners from New York."

It will be observed that in the reasons assigned above for the contemplated amalgamation, the embarrassment arising from the want of funds is stated as common to both the conferring parties, and that not so much as an intimation is given that one party was more in debt than the other, or had experienced more difficulty in meeting its engagements. The general reason assigned for uniting the institutions is contained in the specification immediately preceding the last two. The present writer, however, did not then, nor at any time since, believe it to be a well-founded opinion that "The objects, principles, and operations of both [the conferring parties] are so entirely similar that there can be no good reason assigned for maintaining two." He distinctly made known this conviction to Mr. Evarts, then the Corresponding Secretary of the American Board, in an interview had with him on the subject, and plainly intimated to him that many members of the Presbyterian Church would be found to be of the same mind with the speaker, and that they never would be fully satisfied till they saw a Foreign Missionary Society established in the Church of their preference, founded on its distinctive principles, and exclusively directed by its own members. Still it is not questioned that those who assigned the reasons recited above, did honestly believe in their truth and validity; and that some of the concerned are, to the present time, fully of the opinion that the existence and character of the American Board renders unnecessary and inexpedient a separate organization in the Presbyterian Church.

It ought to be particularly noticed, that it is here stated that these reasons for an amalgamation of the two institutions, were those which were adduced by the Commissioners themselves; and that they were stated, first to a Committee of the Board, and afterwards repeated to the Board itself.

The report of the committee, mentioned in the closing paragraph of the foregoing extended quotation, and which was adopted by the American Board, contained five preliminary terms as conditions of the contemplated union, and seven permanent terms of Union. Neither of these series of terms can be given *in extenso* in this limited sketch; nor, if it were practicable, would there be any use in the insertion of the whole. Of the preliminary terms the second and fourth stand thus:

"2. During the interval which must elapse between the present time and May next, the Directors of the United Foreign Missionary Society will make all practicable exertions to replenish its treasury, so that should the proposed union take place, the engagements to be assumed by the American Board of Commissioners for Foreign Missions may be as few and as small as possible.

"4. The Directors of the United Foreign Missionary Society will direct the missionaries of the several stations not to enter on any new measures involving expense, and generally to practice the strictest economy, till the result of this proposed measure shall be known."

These articles are quoted because it may be thought that they militate with what has been said relative to the debt of the United Foreign Missionary Society. But do they, in reality, contain anything more than a precautionary measure, which might have been entirely proper if no debt whatever of the Society had existed? Still, as the fact was that a debt was known to exist, it is readily admitted that these articles were calculated to prevent its increase, and to provide for its diminution. To get rid of their debt has not been denied to have been one reason why the Directors of the United Foreign Missionary Society were desirous to transfer it to the American Board. That it was not the only, nor the chief reason, that their offer was made and accepted, has, it is believed, been fully shown.

Of the permanent terms of union, agreed upon by the American Board and the "Commissioners from the United Foreign Missionary Society, the Rev. Dr. Thomas A. McAuley, the Rev. Dr. William McMurray, and the Rev. James C. Crane," the sixth article was as follows:

"6. The highest judicatories of the Presbyterian Church, and of the Reformed Dutch Church, will recommend the American Board of Commissioners for Foreign Missions as a national institution, and entitled to the warm support and efficient patronage of the churches under their respective jurisdictions."

This article is inserted, that it may be compared with what was done in relation to it, by the two judicatories to which it refers. The whole action of the General Assembly of the Presbyterian Church on this important subject, after referring it to a Committee, is embraced in the following short extract from their records: "The report of the Committee on a communication from a Committee of the managers of the United Foreign Missionary Society, was taken up, and after mature deliberation it was

"*Resolved*, That the General Assembly do consent to the amalgamation of the American Board of Commissioners for Foreign Missions, and the United Foreign Missionary Society.

"*Resolved further*, That this General Assembly recommend the American Board of Commissioners for Foreign Missions to the favorable notice and Christian support of the Church and people under their care."

FOREIGN OR HEATHEN MISSIONS. 61

The action of the General Synod of the Reformed Dutch Church, on the same subject, is recorded on their minutes as follows:

"WHEREAS, A Committee from the Board of the United Foreign Missionary Society did enter into preliminary arrangements for amalgamating the United Foreign Missionary Society with the American Board of Commissioners for Foreign Missions; and, whereas, it is expressly declared that no pledge of support or recommendation to the patronage of our churches is understood to be implied in the consent of this Synod; therefore,

"*Resolved*, That this Synod consent to transfer the interest of the United Foreign Missionary Society to the American Board of Commissioners for Foreign Missions."

Thus it appears that the sixth article of the permanent terms of union agreed upon by the American Board of Commissioners for Foreign Missions and the Commissioners of the United Foreign Missionary Society was not sanctioned or agreed to by either of the highest judicatories of the churches to which it was submitted. Neither of these judicatories would consent to recommend, or in any manner recognize the American Board as "a national institution"; nor would either of them declare that this Board was "entitled to the warm support and efficient patronage of the churches under their respective jurisdictions." The Synod of the Dutch Church would not so much as recommend the Board in any manner whatever, and state on their minutes that it is expressly declared that no pledge of support or recommendation to the patronage of our churches is understood to be implied in the consent of this Synod to the proposed amalgamation. The General Assembly of the

Presbyterian Church did go so far as to recommend the Board, but only in the same manner in which they have recommended several other benevolent institutions and enterprises. The discussion which took place in the General Assembly, when the subject of amalgamation was under consideration, has been reported and published by one who was a member of the Assembly at the time, and who took part in the debate which ensued; and as this report assigns some reasons for the course pursued, and shows the state of feeling among the members of the Assembly on the occasion; and inasmuch as there have been misapprehensions and erroneous statements in regard to this important transaction, it is believed to be proper to insert the brief report referred to; it is as follows:

"The Committee appointed by the Assembly on the application of the United Foreign Missionary Society, of which Dr. Richards was the chairman, brought in this resolution for adoption:

"*Resolved*, That the General Assembly do approve of the amalgamation of the American Board of Commissioners for Foreign Missions and the United Foreign Missionary Society, on the terms agreed upon."

Dr. Janeway moved to strike out the term which was intended to bind the Assembly to recommend the American Board as a National Society. He assigned as reasons: 1. That such a recommendation would be offensive to other denominations. 2. That if the three denominations embraced by the United Foreign Missionary Society were, sincerely and universally, to act with the American Board, they would not constitute a majority of the religious public in this country; and consequently, if the Assembly were to denominate them a National Society, they would not speak according to fact, and would dishonor themselves by uttering what was not true. Dr. Alexander suggested the striking out of all the terms; Dr. Janeway was deliberating whether it were expedient to make this motion, and still occupying the floor, when Mr. Z. Lewis, one of the managers of the United Foreign Missionary Society, and one of the Committee to obtain the Assembly's sanction to the plan of amalgamation, hastily rose by his side and made the motion. Dr. Janeway then said, "Moderator, I accept that as my motion," and took his seat. The motion was carried, and thus by a formal vote all the terms were stricken out of the resolution. Dr. Neil endeavored to procure a reconsideration of the vote, but failed. Dr. Ely then moved to strike out the words "approve of," and to insert the words "consent to." This motion was carried, and then the resolution read as it now stands in the minutes of the Assembly:

"*Resolved*, That the General Assembly do consent to the amalgamation of the American Board of Commissioners for Foreign Missions and the United Foreign Missionary Society."

When an important article in a contemplated treaty, or agreement of any kind, is rejected by one of the negotiating parties, the other party is, of course, released from all obligation to abide by any other of the proposed stipulations. When, therefore, the two ecclesiastical judicatories, to which the permanent terms of union had been submitted, pointedly rejected the sixth article, and with it, necessarily, everything of which it was the basis in the other articles, the American Board was freed from every moral bond to adhere to any part of the projected agreement. In a word, it became perfectly optional with that Board to take or to refuse the proffered missions. The Board chose to receive them, and it is not seen how it could have done otherwise, in consistency with what it had from its origin openly proclaimed. It was its avowed aim, indicated by its very name, to become a National Institution. But it could not become so in fact without, at least, possessing the superintendence of the Foreign Missions in the Presbyterian and Dutch Churches. Here, then, were nearly all the heathen Missions that had been originated by these churches, now at the offer of the Board, and which, if this Board did not assume them, would certainly be prosecuted by some other agency; for they were of too promising a character to admit a thought of their being abandoned. The property, moreover, which they had accumulated was far more than an equivalent for the debts they had contracted. These debts, amounting as stated to ten thousand dollars, an authentic document now before the writer shows, did not exceed the value of the Maumee Mission alone:

"The Board of Trust of the Synod of Pittsburgh were led, from various considerations, to make additional purchases of land, until, at the time of the transfer (in the autumn of 1825), they possessed upwards of six hundred acres, valued at ten thousand dollars. This land, which was recently, if it is not still, in the possession of the American Board, lies immediately adjoining the Wabash and Lake Erie Canal, and as the Indian claims have been now entirely extinguished, it must prove extremely valuable to the Board."—*Manuscript statement from Rev. E. P. Swift, of the date of February 8, 1838.*

"I remember most distinctly to have heard Mr. Evarts say, that his Board had received from the United Foreign Missionary Society, such an amount of property as ought to prevent any mention ever being made of the debts transferred, as being a burden."—*Quotation from a letter of Rev. Dr. Samuel Miller, dated January* 8, 1838.

The American Board, therefore acted wisely, and in perfect accordance with its own long cherished purposes and hopes, in assuming these missions; although the terms which the Commissioners of the United Foreign Missionary Society had proposed and agreed to do, were not sanctioned, but refused, by the judicatories which had a perfect and acknowledged right to reject them.

It is believed that the only heathen mission in the Presbyterian Church, which was not transferred to the American Board, along with those already mentioned, was one which was under the supervision of the Synod of South Carolina and Georgia, namely: Mission among the Chickasaw Indians.

MISSION AMONG THE CHICKASAW INDIANS. This Synod, it appears, some time previously to the transfer, had established a mission among the Chickasaws; whose country was included within the chartered limits of the States of Mississippi and Alabama. The Rev. T. C. Steward was employed for some time as a stated missionary among these Indians. A promising school was opened, and considerable anxiety was awakened among the pagans for the instruction of their children. But the want of authentic information prevents the insertion in this sketch of further details in regard to this mission; except that it appears to have been resigned to the American Board in the year 1828.

[The foregoing accounts may be supplemented in some particulars, from the Minutes, in manuscript, of the Western Missionary Society's Board of Trust: 1. This Board of Trust, January 2, 1821, adopted a Minute which opened the way for co-operation with the United

Foreign Missionary Society, and proposed a joint effort of the two Societies to form a new mission among the Indians,—in a manner suggested. No further reference to this matter is found in the Board of Trust's Minutes, nor any in the publications of the United Foreign Missionary Society.

2. The next references to this subject are in the same MS. Volume of Minutes, in 1825, April 12, June 12, June 27, and October 25, and in the Minutes of the Synod of Pittsburgh, October 27, 1825. These Minutes show that a complete transfer of the work and property of the Board of Trust, W. M. S., was made to the United Foreign Missionary Society. A reference to compensation for the property transferred is made in the Minutes of the Board of Trust of June 27, 1825, to the payment of $1,000 by the United Foreign Missionary Society to the Board of Trust, W. M. S., without particulars, but probably to provide for certain contingent debts. The property at the Maumee station thus transferred was of considerable value, the land alone being estimated at $10,000.

3. The local and personal interest of this singular transfer has passed away, but it suggests two general remarks:

1. The *Union* feature of the Society to which the Synod of Pittsburgh's Missions were transferred. It was in theory a Presbyterian Church Society; otherwise no transfer would have been made; but it was a *united* Society, "composed of the Presbyterian, the Reformed Dutch, and the Associate Reformed Churches, and all others who may choose to join them." If well-ordered in method as in object, and conducted with efficiency, this Society might be expected to become a great and blessed Church movement for the conversion of the

world. Such no doubt was the purpose of its founders. And its influence at home would have been great and practical in the lines of Christian fellowship between the three kindred Churches,—fellowship not only beneficial, but delightful. Alas, for its short life! And wherefore?

2. In reply—the painful historical events to which attention has been called on preceding pages, go far to account for its short course. Besides these events, the Constitution of the Society contained two things that rendered its success uncertain. One was apparent in its Fifth Article, see page 39, *supra*, which specified a pecuniary qualification for membership, and a larger sum of money for a seat and right to vote in its Board of Managers. We find nothing of this kind in the Missions of the Apostolic Church, nor in the Scriptural principles on which they were conducted.

The other discouraging feature is the lack of a closer connection between the Society and the three Churches. The Fourth Article specifies that the annual report of the Board of the Society is to be "presented to the highest judicatory of the three denominations, for their information." This article, and especially its last three words, seem to be the only proviso for *the review and control* of the Society by the three Churches. The Society itself was constituted not by the judicatories, but as noted above by pecuniary payments for membership as well as officers. Even so great and serious a matter as the transfer of the missions to another Board seems to have been virtually done by the Society, rather than by the Churches. Many able and good men were members of these three denominations then, as there are now; but the lessons of experience were then inadequately understood. The connection of our divinely

appointed Church government with the work of
Christian missions needs to be carefully studied. Its
principles are generally applicable to practical cases; its
rules of procedure may vary with Providential circumstances. We may believe, however, that the unhappy
ending of the Society's life, after its work so full of
promise, and supported by the sympathy, gifts, and
prayers of so many of the excellent of the earth, did
nevertheless become an important means of a greater
work of foreign missions at an early day.]

SYNODICAL MISSIONS.

[THE Note here inserted refers particularly to missions, domestic and foreign, which were conducted by several Synods of the Church, in their separate organization. These were conducted with the approval of the General Assembly—by its "direction and allowance," indeed at its request in some cases. Lessons of interest may be drawn from their proceedings in 1789-1811, 1791-1813, and 1802-1826, respectively, as bearing on the general missionary work of the present day—1892—its principles being the same.

Only three of the Synods may here be referred to, but the sphere of action in the case of the second was not exclusively missionary.

THE SYNOD OF VIRGINIA. The Synod of Virginia held its first meeting in 1788. Its boundaries included Virginia, Western Pennsylvania, Ohio—then extending indefinitely westward, and Kentucky. Its evangelistic work reached many new settlements of white people on the frontiers, many colored people, and several remnants of Indian tribes. In 1789 this Synod felt moved to undertake missionary work, additional to the missions of the General Assembly, but no doubt with its warm approval, and it organized *The Commission of Synod* to carry into effect the Synod's *Plan of Missions and its Rules*. The Commission consisted of four ministers and as many elders, one of them acting as Treasurer. Collections were taken in the churches for its work, and encouragement attended its labors. It missionaries were required to be unordained and unmarried men, and were usually probationers for the ministry, who had been recommended for appointment by their Presbyteries. There were then no Theological Seminaries, and no students with vacations available for short periods of service. These 'Commission' missionaries were usually appointed for a year, on suitable salaries, and were left under the supervision of their Presbyteries respectively. The restrictive rule as to marriage was not waived apparently, but enforced by the discontinuance of appointment, in the only instance specified in the Minutes now accessible, "as he did not answer the purposes of the Commission"; but with no unkind feeling. The rule was no doubt regarded as suited to a new country and its itinerant work.

The missions of the Commission were commended by the General Assembly, which referred specially to its having "paid attention to Indian tribes on the frontiers." But it was difficult to obtain missionaries for the increasing population, white, colored in some parts of its bounds, and Indians, and difficult also to obtain pecuniary means for their support. After some years the Commission was divided into two sections, "under the names of the Commission East of the Alleghany and the Commission West, acting with great efficiency." Missionaries were sent also to Kentucky, where a noble work was begun, with not a little self-denial. But in 1807 under the pressure of growing labors and inadequate means, the Synod expressed to the General Assembly its purpose to resign the missionary work. The Assembly requested the Synod to continue in the charge of it for the present. "After a few years, the Synodical Commission ceased, and the Assembly conducted its work by a Board appointed for the purpose." These notices are taken from the Minutes of the General Assembly and from Dr. W. H. Foote's Sketches of Virginia, in 1850. Dr. Foote also says that "the Minutes of the Commission for some years are supposed to be irrecoverably lost." Some of the most useful and eminent men in our ministry, the Rev. Archibald Alexander, D.D., and others, began their public labors for Christ under the care of this Commission, or Standing Committee of the Synod on Missions.

THE SYNOD OF THE CAROLINAS. The Synod of the Carolinas, organized in 1788, appointed a *Standing Commission* in 1791. It was a general Commission, in charge of all matters of Synodical business when the Synod was not in session, and its decision was final. It took a warm interest in the religious instruction of the Catawba Indians for two years; but the Indians "became weary of it," and further work for them appears to have been relinquished. The Commission aided in the support of domestic missionaries in the three States of North and South Carolina, and Georgia, and also in territories farther south and southwest—as far distant as Natchez in the territory of Mississippi. In this missionary work the Synod complied with the directions of the General Assembly; but eventually by overture the work was placed again in the charge of the Assembly. In 1813 the Synod was divided, three Presbyteries constituting the Synod of North Carolina, and as many forming the Synod of South Carolina and Georgia. Missionary labors were still encouraged in both these Synods, but so far as appears not by organized Commissions for that purpose. But the Synod of South Carolina and Georgia supported a mission among the Chickasaw Indians—referred to on page 65, *supra*.

At a far later period the Synods of Virginia and of North Carolina formed the *Central Board of Foreign Missions;* and the Synods of South Carolina and Georgia, and of Tennessee, formed the *Southern Board of Foreign Missions;* both these Boards being in friendly co-operation with the American Board of Foreign Missions. No particular account need be given here of their work in connection with the American Board. In 1838, these Boards—the Central and the Southern—transferred their relations to the Board of Foreign Missions of the General Assembly. Cordial Christian regard and sympathy, as well as a recognition of the responsibility of the Church, no doubt marked all these proceedings.

THE SYNOD OF PITTSBURGH. The Synod of Pittsburgh was constituted by the General Assembly in 1802. Its three Presbyteries,—Redstone, Ohio, and Erie,—had been connected with the Synod of Virginia. Its territory was chiefly Western Pennsylvania, but included parts of Western Virginia and of Eastern Ohio, as it does to this day. Its vigorous people, mostly of Scotch-Irish stock, had come from Eastern Pennsylvania, Maryland, and Central Virginia. This Synod signalized its advent by organizing itself at its first meeting in 1802 as *The Western Missionary Society.* The Society appointed a *Board of Trust,* which was afterwards chartered by the State, and which consisted of six ministers and three elders. This Board elected annually from its members a Chairman, a Secretary, and a Treasurer.* The Minutes of the Society and of its Board were kept in the same volume, separate from the Minutes of the Synod, and were laid before the Synod annually for its review and control. The members and officers of the Board were usually re-elected. Among them were some of the most excellent and leading men of their day in the Western Church.

* All unsalaried, as in the Commission of Virginia.

SYNODICAL MISSIONS. 73

The Synod conducted its missionary work with vigor and success, as related by Dr. Green, until its Indian or Foreign Missions were unhappily transferred to the United Foreign Missionary Society in 1825. Its much larger work in the home field passed into the charge of the Board of Domestic Missions, General Assembly, in the next year, 1826.

THE INDIAN MISSIONS. The Indian Missions of these Synods were regarded as *Foreign*. Such was the *usus loquendi*. Of course they were also considered as missions to the Heathen. The Indians were foreigners in their language, way of life, religious usages, treatment by the Government in waging wars and forming treaties with them. They are now called the wards of the Government, and a liberal and kind policy is adopted concerning them. The policy of the General Government towards them was always humane, whatever may have been their treatment by some of the border States. But even to this day many of the tribes require too often the control of the army. It is only the Gospel that can make them citizens. They may enjoy for their children the benefits of common schools, as do other children; but for adults the missionary who knows their language thoroughly, and who remains in their service for life, Providence permitting, is as much needed as his brethren are by Hindus or Koreans. David Brainerd, Cyrus Kingsbury, Dr. Williamson, and others still living were foreign missionaries, and were so considered, not less than Henry Martyn, of India, or Dr. Morrison, of China.

These views, in general, were held in these Synods, and all the more strongly because of the great wrongs perpetrated on the Indian tribes by lawless white people. But in the period here referred to, and especially in the bounds of these Synods, only feeble and fragmentary bands of Indians were usually within reach. For them earnest efforts were made to promote the knowledge of the Gospel and its civilization, as shown elsewhere in this volume. The Wyandots, and the Ottawas, of Northeastern Ohio, the Cornplanter villages of Senecas, on the borders of Pennsylvania and New York, others by missionaries of the Virginia and Southern Synods, and particularly by the Rev. Gideon Blackburn, under the direction of the General Assembly, were the subjects of deep sympathy; and self-sacrificing labors were made for their benefit. By the Synod of Pittsburgh, teachers were employed, both men and women, and laborers to train the Indians in farming and other kinds of work. Visits were made to the Indian settlements by ministers of churches within reach of them, occupying several days of travelling on horseback, at times through the almost unbroken wilderness. Many such visits by leading pastors were made for considerable periods by such men as Messrs. Dodd, McCurdy, Hughes, Tait, and shorter visits at the request of the Synod's Board of Trust by Messrs. Anderson, Marquis, McPherrin, Herron, Swift, Patterson, Stevenson, Satterfield, and others. Their own churches were supplied by neighboring pastors, the ministers generally being in sympathy with their brethren, and their congregations also. Mr. Tait's absence for several months, as provisional superintendent of the Maumee Mission, was at the request of the Synod, which directed the Presbytery to take the charge of supplying his pulpit. Early in this century Mr. Dodd spent several years in this service under the direction of the Board of Trust, but following his own convictions of duty. Mr. Badger, one of the most remarkable men, spent some years subsequent to 1806; Mr. McCurdy was eminent in his Indian labors (see his Memoirs by Dr. Elliott). Dr. McCurdy's Biography refers to his travelling 4,500 miles as member of the Board of Trust and for twelve years its Treasurer, and on repeated visits to the Indian missions, spending a year on one of these visits, "travelling not in steamboats, railroad cars, or stage coaches, protected from the weather, but on horseback, in all seasons of the year, over poor roads, swamps, and rivers, often encountering much difficulty and no common fatigue and exposure." Dr. McCurdy continued in the charge of his first and only church, with its full sympathy, for over thirty years, until his health required him to withdraw from active labors. Notwithstanding his abundant work for the Board of Trust and for the Indians, and many evangelistic visits to new settlements, his own "country" congregation steadily increased in numbers, strength, and spiritual life and vigor. Not a few were the pastors of churches in this Synod, who were men of like character and usefulness.

THE DOMESTIC MISSIONS. The Domestic Missions of these Synods, already referred to by Dr. Green, and in the former part of these Notes, should have further attention relating chiefly to this work in the Synod of Pittsburgh. Within one or two hundred miles of its chief town, the population was rapidly increasing. Most of the new-coming people were of Presbyterian preferences. They were mostly poor in their circumstances, but with good habits and industry they were gradually becoming "well off." Many of the families were anxious to enjoy church privileges, and many of them were good judges of good preaching. Usually they needed assistance, however, from the Synod's Board for a time. It was evidently important to secure the appointment of educated ministers as pastors and evangelists, men sound in the faith, of preaching ability, and of earnestness. And it was encouraging that many such ministers became available.

The Board of Trust's commission to its missionaries was usually for short periods, probably on account of its limited funds; but renewable without difficulty if funds were forthcoming, and if congregations offered according to their ability to provide in part the required support. This line of procedure tended to promote a settled ministry in the churches. It also served to test the adaptation of ministers to special fields of labor. Some ministers had to work on farms for their support, while they preached on the Sabbath in feeble churches or as opportunity offered, and thereby aided in collecting congregations of which they became pastors, while their week-day labors tended to provide for their families and for themselves in their old age. In addition to the Board's evangelists, the pastors of the stronger churches in many cases made evangelizing journeys, to preach in new settlements and in locations by the wayside. Several notices of such evangelizing work are found in the missionary records of those years. Another may be added here:

A few years ago a retired merchant in New York, an elder in one of the principal churches, asked the writer of these Notes if he had ever heard of a Mr. Tait, a preacher in Western Pennsylvania? "O yes, I knew him well. He was often a guest at my father's house—he with others on their journeys to Synods or meetings of Presbytery. He was one of the best preachers." "Well," said this gentleman, "to him I owe my being led to Christ as my Saviour." He was then a young man from the East, on a visit to a family of his friends or relatives at a small lumber station on the Alleghany

River. Mr. Tait, like others of his brethren, had left his church on a short tour to districts as yet unsupplied with Gospel privileges. Travelling on horseback, he stopped at this river settlement near the end of the week, some thirty miles from his home. There he preached to a few people on the Sabbath, administered the sacrament of the Lord's Supper to some communicants, and early in the next week went on his way. Among his hearers was this young man. Now in his declining years, after a life of active service for our blessed Lord, he still cherished the memory of the good and faithful minister. A son and a grandson of the venerable elder are esteemed and useful Presbyterian ministers.

WOMEN'S WORK. Among the best supporters of these missions were the women of the churches. In those early days and in a new and sparsely settled country, where ordinary business was chiefly conducted by barter and but little money was available, their missionary gifts were in many cases the work of their own hands. By weaving, knitting, and sewing, in the use of flax and wool; in preparing articles of food that admitted of transportation in a rough way; in readiness to go as missionary teachers and helpers at Indian stations, when Providence permitted; above all in the great, if not the greatest, agency of prayer for the divine blessing on this evangelizing work—in all such ways their interest in its success was very manifest. And when pecuniary means were available, who could be more liberal in their gifts? The meetings for prayer were often largely their meetings, then as now. All praise for their labors, all honor to their memory!

In looking over the acknowledgment of receipts by the W. F. M. Society, in the *Missionary Chronicle*, nearly sixty years ago, one cannot but notice the number and the variety of the gifts of both women and children to the foreign missionary cause, then just organized by the Synod. Female Auxiliary Society, Female Sewing Society, Female Benevolent Society, Female Missionary Society, Ladies of —— Church, names often repeated, and also many anonymous gifts of articles of jewelry, and gifts of needle and knitting work,—*e. g.*, " 26 pairs of socks, not valued," for an Indian mission, etc., were the sources of many gifts. In far the most cases the donations of the women were united with those of the men in church collections. Gifts of Sunday-schools, of several children, of children in a family, of a boy or a girl, were also frequently acknowledged. And in both these classes of acknowledgments, two things are noticeable: 1st, that they were given directly to the Board; and 2d, that, with the exception of women's donations to constitute Pastors Honorary Members, the donors hardly ever desired a special object, with a letter or a report in reply.

There was, however, no general organization of the women of the Church in those days, in a few large Boards, such as are now the auxiliaries of the Foreign Board, G. A.—auxiliaries doing a noble work in the cause of missions. Their great work, great it surely is, has been so ordered as to preserve its relations to the General Assembly through the Foreign Board, G. A. This is done by reserving to the Assembly's Board: 1st, the appointment of missionaries; 2d, the designation of their mission or field of labor; and 3d, the amount of their salary, making it uniform with that of their sister missionaries. Under these rules the executive officers are always happy to be aided by the counsels and the information of the auxiliary Boards; while the work in the field abroad is sufficiently unified, and all parties at home are responsible and loyal to the Church. Should modifications of this line of policy at any time seem to be required, the public opinion of the friends of missions can readily find expression through our General Assembly.

To these general statements of Women's Work in Synodical Missions may be added a beautiful incident, which years ago came to the knowledge of the writer, and which occurred in one of these Synods—an example in its spirit which could no doubt be verified in cases not a few. The lovely daughter of an eminent clergyman, early in this century, married a farmer's son, who was every way worthy of her, and the marriage was a blessed one. They were not rich in this world's goods; he was a teacher of a common school, which yielded but little support, but he could add something to their comfort by odds and ends of work in the small town, while she was the only indoor member of the family. He pursued certain studies, and became qualified for a wider sphere of life; while she found loving work in the charge of her children, though still with almost no domestic assistance. Several years passed. A happier and more loving family could seldom be found, and they were now in moderate but comfortable circumstances. During an absence of some months from his home, and thinking of the goodness of God to his household, so largely owing to his beloved wife, he felt moved to send her a gift of $100— a large sum for them; but wishing to learn what would be most acceptable to her, if expended in the large city where he was then on a visit, he wrote to her of his purpose, with affectionate references to the goodness of God to them and their children, which had followed her loving and gentle home life. Her reply was worthy of them both, while it showed the chief end of her wishes. She could not be too grateful for her husband's invariable love and kindness. She needed no additional evidence of it; but as he had so generously thought of her, as many times before, she would suggest that his handsome gift should be sent to the ——Board of Foreign Missions. And this was done, though he had already made his usual and liberal remittance for that year to its funds.

The records of these Synodical Missions show:

1. That in their origin, supervision, administration, and control, they were all in the charge of the Synods. They were Church Missions, not Voluntary Society Missions.

2. That in their beginning they antedated the leading Missionary Boards of our time. They had their Commission, Society, or Board, elected annually by the Synods; their Board of Trust in one case, or Executive Committee; their Chairman, sometimes called President in the Minutes; their Secretary; their Treasurer; all elected annually. They met at stated and frequent times; they kept regular Minutes of their proceedings; they made Annual Reports of their work to the Synods, for review and control. Their first dates of meeting were 1789 and 1802, respectively. The earliest of the leading Missionary Boards in this country was formed in 1810; and the Foreign Board of the General Assembly, in 1837.

3. That for defraying the expenses of their work they depended mainly on the gifts of the churches, and these were bestowed with little external pressure. A wise economy was observed in all administrative expenditures; the executive officers set a good example in this respect. Seldom were collecting agents employed; rarely were special objects allotted to particular donors.

Appeals directly to the churches for the support of the work were made by their pastors, under the sanction of the Synods and Presbyteries, and thereby means were obtained for the support of the missions. It was on the principle of Christian stewardship, and the belief that giving is the fruit of divine grace. As the result of this belief the duty was recognized that liberal giving was to be promoted by the use of the means of grace— the Word, Sacraments, and Prayer. The teaching of the Word did not undervalue the use of information, much less the labors of pastors in their own pulpits and by exchange with each other, by missionary sermons at Presbyteries and Synods, as well as at other religious services. Not much reliance was placed on new measures, nor was any disparaging references made to the methods of preceding years. The ministers were men in earnest. They preached the Scripture doctrines of their Church without toning them down. The elders and members of their churches were in sympathy with their teachers. All relied on the regular means of grace, as appointed by God, and as leading to obedience to His commandments—the last included.

4. That great success was given to these missions. In foreign or heathen missions but limited results were obtained in some cases, though with encouragement in others. But the experience acquired bore good fruit a few years later in the organization of the Western Foreign Missionary Society. Its origin resulted from the principles, policy, methods, and the work itself of these Synodical Missions. And as it was, in successful work, transferred to the General Assembly, with its missions, property, and evident proofs of the blessing of God, its history may be referred to as closely connected with the great and almost world-wide work of Missions

of the Presbyterian Church, down to the present day.

5. For the Domestic Missions of these Synods, let a brief summary statement bear witness to their success. The splendid country within a hundred miles of the chief town in one of the Synods gradually became well settled, and its people generally able to live in comfortable circumstances. Then with equal steps were multiplied churches, schools, colleges, theological seminaries, female seminaries; clerical, legal, and medical men—well educated, and women of superior education; law, order; towns, villages; prospering industries —especially in agricultural and mining lines, manufactures, commerce, steamboats, railways; hospitals, orphan asylums, public libraries—almost every fruit of Christian civilization. The small town, originally but a fort for the protection of its few people, became a city of 238,000 by the late census, or of over 700,000 people in its immediate suburbs and its county.

All these prospering conditions are the harvest of the grain of mustard-seed. Thanks for the early and humble work of Christian Missions! Thanks above all for the blessing of God on the preaching of the Gospel!

This Note may suggest two remarks, both relating to essential subjects. *First*, the system of doctrines held by these Synods; and *Second*, the connection of church government with their missions. Only brief statements can be given to each.

1st. As to the Doctrines, the Synods stood on the old rock of faith, as presented by Christ himself (John iii. 14–17; Matthew xxii. 14; Luke iv. 16–30). The creed of their members and supporters was that of their Church, as expressed in the Westminster Confession of

Faith. Some of its great truths as bearing on the subject of Christian Missions: 1. The sovereign, electing, holy purpose of God—from eternity to eternity. 2. The fallen, sinful, perishing, and hopeless condition of all men. 3. The infinite love and grace of God, the blessed Trinity, as manifested in redemption. But all, without succession in the mind of God.

The highest motives for complying with the will of God, revealed to his disciples by Jesus Christ: 1. His last commandment. 2. Compassion for lost souls. 3. Assurance of final success, by the power of the Holy Spirit, to accompany the preaching of the Gospel to every creature. 4. The promise of the Saviour's presence with His disciples in the fulfilment of His commission, even unto the end of the world. And so the work of Christian Missions shall end with the universal reign of grace.

It may be confidently affirmed that not a minister nor an elder could be found in these Synods, who would not avow his faith in these divinely revealed doctrines and motives. All was harmony in doctrinal belief.

2d. As to Church order, subsidiary to the Doctrines, but also of Scripture warrant: 1. The Church itself a missionary organization. 2. Its ministry called and commissioned by God, ordinarily at the request of His people. 3. Official parity of rank maintained among the members of this ministry. 4. Churches organized, and united under the care of Councils or Presbyteries, —not independent of each other nor dependent on but one overseer. 5. Ruling Elders, and a Minister, one or more, chosen by the communicants; their action open to review by the Presbytery. 6. Deacons, when needed. 7. Representative Presbyteries or Councils constituted, equally of ministers and elders, with authoritative but limited power, and subject to appeal to the chief Assembly.

These *principles* of church and missionary order remain steadfast, the same for the Presbyterian Church now, in every country, as for the Apostolic churches of Jerusalem, Antioch, or Ephesus; but the *application* of these principles may vary in some respects, according to Providential conditions as to time, place, or manner. They are not held by our Christian people in such a sense as would hinder the missionary work of Christian brethren of other churches. But as Christ Jesus is the great Representative of His people in every denomination, and their Surety in the Covenant of Grace, so His redeemed people may represent Him in the common work of evangelization according to the light given unto them severally in Holy Scripture, with charity and sympathy each for all.

No enlarged treatment of these subjects is in place here, but they all point to Christ, as our all in all in the work of missions.]

When the General Assembly reorganized their Board of Missions, in 1828, they declared, as has been shown, that it was authorized to conduct Foreign as well as Domestic Missions; and, for a time, both these objects commanded the earnest attention of the Executive Committee. A well qualified exploring missionary to Greece was appointed, and for a short time sanguine hopes were entertained that he would fulfil his appointment. Eventually, however, he declined it, on considerations which were satisfactory to the Committee. An attempt was subsequently made to establish a mission among the Chippeway Indians. An exploring agent was appointed, in whose behalf governmental influence was obtained, and who spent more than a year in the service of the

Board. But it was found that the American Board, by extending, as was then in contemplation, the operations of its establishment at Mackinaw, could most advantageously take cognizance of this field of missionary enterprise, and to that Board the field was accordingly resigned. By this time, the prosecution of domestic missions had become so extensive and onerous, that the opinion generally obtained, among the friends of the General Assembly's Board, that till a separate institution should be organized in the Presbyterian Church, for the sole management of Foreign Missions, the existing institution would better confine its measures to the Home department; and leave Foreign operations to the American Board, with which a considerable portion of the Presbyterian Church was now co-operating.

MISSION AT BUENOS AYRES. It was, for a time, confidently expected by the friends of Orthodox piety in the United States, as well as in Europe, that the Revolution in South America would open a door for the propagation of the Protestant religion; and sanguine hopes were entertained of the happy effects that were speedily to result, from the free circulation of the Bible, and the unobstructed labors of missionaries, in that extensive region; in which the Romish superstition had so long and so oppressively prevailed. Time and experience, if they have not entirely blasted these hopes and expectations, have proved that the period at which they are to be realized is yet future. What was done by the Presbyterian Church for the propagation of evangelical truth, may be learned from the following extract from the *Christian Advocate*, for the month of January, 1828. The article from which our extract is made, partakes of the delusion then prevalent, and is headed—"A Presbytery in Buenos

Ayres." The editor says: "We have before us a letter from the Rev. Theophilus Parvin to the Presbytery of Philadelphia, dated 'Buenos Ayres, April 17th, 1827': Mr. Parvin was ordained as a missionary by the Presbytery of Philadelphia, in January, 1826; and since that time has been enrolled as one of the members of that body. About a month after his ordination, he sailed for Buenos Ayres with his wife, a daughter of Mr. Rodney, the American minister, who died at that place. Early in the following April, as appears by the letter before us, he arrived in safety at the place of his destination. Since that time he has been diligently occupied in missionary labors. Having determined entirely to support himself, a considerable portion of his time has been unavoidably spent in teaching. Soon after his arrival at Buenos Ayres, he received the appointment of 'Professor of Greek and English,' in the university established in that city. This appointment he resigned last autumn; finding that he could dispense with its emoluments, and desirous to secure more time for ministerial labors. His chief reliance for support at present is on a flourishing academy which he has established, containing, at the last account, about fifty scholars. He has also established, in concert with Miss McMullin, who accompanied him from the United States for the purpose, a promising female academy, to which some of his attention is devoted. While these institutions afford an income adequate to all the wants of his family, they are in fact directly subservient to his missionary views. They promote knowledge, and prepare for the reception of evangelical instruction. He has preached regularly, first in his academy, and lately in a large room, selected and fitted up for the purpose. A chapel is greatly needed, and efforts are making to prepare one. The Lord's Supper has been administered three times a year—the first time to eight communicants, the second to six, the third to nine, and the last time to thirteen. He has administered the sacrament of Baptism only in three instances. He had, at the time of writing his letter, celebrated marriage six times. A Bible Society and a Missionary Society have been established, which meet monthly. A flourishing Sabbath-school, of one hundred and seven scholars, is also established—it is well attended and increasing. The foregoing statement is derived from Mr. Parvin's communication to the Presbytery, in connection with a private letter which we have seen from Mr. Torrey. Mr. Parvin's letter concludes as follows: 'In conclusion, I am happy in being able to say, that in my academical and clerical labors, I have for the last six weeks been favored with the valuable services of the Rev. William Torrey. In consequence of his arrival, and the settlement of the Rev. Mr. Brown, of Scotland, in a village of Scotch emigrants, about twelve miles from the city, we shall probably find it expedient, as soon as we can receive dismissions from the Presbyteries to which we belong, to form a Presbytery in Buenos Ayres. I have therefore to solicit my dismission from your reverend body, with a view to connect myself with a Presbytery to be organized here. The great difficulty of maintaining any intercourse with those at home, because of the close blockade of our port, must serve as my apology for not having forwarded, some months since, a communication of a nature similar to the present.'"

In consequence of the information contained in the letters above mentioned, the Board of Missions of the General Assembly was convened, when two communications from Mr. Torrey, dated August 24th and 25th, were also submitted for consideration, by the members to whom they had been addressed. It appeared that Mr. Torrey was very actively and usefully employed in missionary labors, but that he needed pecuniary assistance. After serious deliberation on the whole subject, a minute was made, of which the following is a transcript:

"Letters were read from Rev. Messrs. Parvin and Torrey, at Buenos Ayres, in South America. Whereupon "*Resolved*, That two hundred dollars be allowed for the assistance of Mr. Torrey, and that Drs. Janeway, Green, and Ely be a committee to select and recommend a suitable person as a missionary to the same region." The editor of the *Advocate* afterwards adds: "We are glad to be able to state that the committee appointed for the purpose have the prospect of engaging a promising young missionary to go to the aid of his brethren at Buenos Ayres."

The sum here mentioned, was carefully expended, in the purchase of clothing for the missionary, Bibles, and other books for the mission, and some articles of furniture, to aid in fitting up an apartment as a place of public worship. The articles were forwarded and arrived in safety. It is believed that the communicants mentioned above, consisted of the mission family and other strangers from Britain and the United States.

Such were the flattering prospects and fond anticipations, which were destined to terminate in utter disappointment. A particular detail of the unpropitious circumstances and causes which occasioned the unhappy result, it is unnecessary, and would be tedious to specify. The amount was—that no additional missionary could at that time be engaged to reinforce the establishment—the female teacher was disappointed in her expectations, and returned to the United States—not long after, Mr. Parvin buried his wife, lost his own health, which he never fully recovered, and returned, with two motherless children, to his native country—every prospect became increasingly dark—no Presbytery was ever formed—and the mission languished, till it became nearly, if not entirely, extinct. Mr. Brown, it is believed, went to Scotland, and afterwards returned, and is now a resident of Buenos Ayres. Mr. Torrey, it is understood, has not long since returned to the United States.

But the failure of this mission might, and probably would have been repaired, by another, better concerted and arranged, had it not, in its progress, and by similar and simultaneous failures of other missionary bodies, shown conclusively, that the causes of disappointment were deeply seated in the state of society and the habits of the people. In a word, the engrossing concerns and scenes of a revolutionary state, the prevalence of infidelity among men of station and liberal knowledge, the general and total ignorance of the nature of religious liberty, the strong remaining influence of bigotry and superstition in the mass of the people, cherished by the deadly hostility to reformation of the larger part of the popish priesthood, rendered it indubitable that changes for the better must be the work of time, be produced by gradual advances, and by the improvement of an ignorant and deeply depraved population.

THREE CLASSES IN FRIENDS OF MISSIONS. It was matter of painful regret to many Presbyterians, both lay and clerical, that for several years in succession, the Church of their preference, although both large and wealthy, had in its distinctive character, no part whatever, so far as the heathen were concerned, in carrying into effect the Saviour's parting command to His disciples, "to teach all nations—to preach the Gospel to every creature." There seem to have been three sections, or classes—not to denominate them parties—in the Presbyterian Church, that differed in their sentiments, relative to the most eligible method of prosecuting foreign missions—all admitting that the duty of sustaining them was important, and obligatory on all Christians. One of these classes considered an ecclesiastical organization, if not essential, yet of such moment, that they would countenance no missionary institution that was otherwise constituted; and therefore would contribute nothing, or very little, to the American Board. When the spirit of missions was first awakened in this country, by what had been done and was still doing in Britain, few had any digested and systematic opinions on the subject. The desire was to promote missionary effort, in any way that appeared practicable. Hence it happened (as in such cases it will always happen) that examination, experience, and observation, led many to change both opinion and action, in regard to the conduct of missions. No inconsiderable number of those who for a time contributed to the American Board, changed their views, and became unwilling to patronize any institution of a missionary kind, which had not an ecclesiastical organization and responsibility.

A second class agreed with the first, in thinking that an ecclesiastical organization was clearly the most Scriptural, and in every view the most desirable. Some of them even declared, that they were penetrated with grief and shame, at seeing the Presbyterian Church so regardless both of duty and reputation, as to neglect to form, and zealously and effectually maintain, a missionary establishment of her own; and they affirmed that they did believe the frown of Zion's King was resting, and would continue to rest on this Church, so long as she continued disobedient to His express command. Still they maintained, that till the Presbyterian Church could be roused to proper action on this important subject, for which they declared they would never cease to pray and labor, it was far better to co-operate with the American Board, than to remain wholly inactive, and do nothing in the great cause of evangelizing the world. They remarked, that although the American Board was a secular institution in its corporate character, and was brought into existence by the agency, and for the special accommodation of congregational and independent churches, yet, for the present, all its concerns were conducted by men of decided piety; that their missionaries also were eminently good and devoted men, and that among them were numbered some of the youth trained at our own theological seminaries; that the measures of the Board were, for the most part, prudently taken and well conducted; that its liberality was such as to enroll several Presbyterians among its corporate, and many among its honorary members; and that God had crowned the missions of this Board with great success. These things considered, the Presbyterians of this class avowed their determination to co-operate, cheerfully and zealously, with the American Board, till an organization which they could fully approve, should be formed in their own Church. Accordingly, those of this class who were members of the Board, often attended its annual meetings, and took an interested and active part in all its proceedings; contributed, and encouraged others to contribute liberally, to its funds; countenanced and assisted its agents; often advocated its cause in Synods, Presbyteries, and congregations; voted in the General Assembly in favor of recommending it to the kindness and patronage of the churches; and manifested toward it every act of friendship in their power, short of taking part in any measure for formally associating the Presbyterian Church with it, as one of its integral and constituent parts; for to this, they declared they were decisively and irreconcilably opposed.

Many individuals of this second class, and probably of the first also, besides the preference which they gave to an ecclesiastical organization, were deliberately of the opinion, that the union of the whole Presbyterian Church with the American Board in missionary concerns, would create a body too large for useful action, especially when they looked forward to the magnitude it would acquire in a short time to come. They thought that the American Board was already as large as it ought to be; and that the Presbyterian Church, if united, would make another body of magnitude sufficient to act with the greatest advantage. This opinion is strongly reinforced by a publication of the Baptist missionaries at Serampore—the result of long experience and close observation. With much in the same strain, they say: "To those who carefully weigh the subject, it will be evident, that there must be limits, beyond which a missionary body can scarcely go, without almost wholly losing its nature, and managing its concerns in quite a secular manner; and when this is the case, the genuine missionary spirit evaporates, and with it the hope of any extensive success." See "Thoughts on the propagation of Christianity more effectually among the Heathen."

The Southern Board of Foreign Missions, composed of the Synods of South Carolina, Georgia, and East Tennessee; and the Central Board, formed by the Synods of Virginia and North Carolina, and both auxiliary to the American Board, appear to have acted on the general principles of this second class of Presbyterians—differing, perhaps, in some shades of opinion. Both these Boards are now looking forward to the period, when, in consistency with existing engagements, they may formally and fully co-operate with the Board of Foreign Missions of the Presbyterian Church.

There was a third class of Presbyterians, who were fully of the opinion that no separate organization was either necessary or expedient in the Presbyterian Church; that every dictate of duty, interest, and a regard to economy, in the expenditure of money collected for missionary purposes, urged to a formal union, or amalgamation of interests and action with the American Board of Commissioners for Foreign Missions; and that the General Assembly ought to adopt the most decisive measures, and use all its influence, to bring out the whole strength of the Presbyterian Church, in support of the measures and operations of that Board. They pleaded, that a large proportion of the Presbyterian population was ardently attached to this Board, constantly received and highly prized its publications, contributed cheerfully to its funds, and would be better pleased with a formal connection with it, than with any other measure or arrangement that could be adopted, in regard to this subject. Many of those who composed this class, if not complete Congregationalists in sentiment, had strong congregational leanings; and others, whose opinions were more strictly Presbyterian, thought that there ought to be no objection to a full concert in action, with a Board in which there were so many members both of the clergy and the laity of their own denomination. If good was done, they thought it a matter of no importance, whether it were done by a secular or an ecclesiastical organization.

It was this class of Presbyterians that attempted, in

the General Assembly of 1826, to obtain the adoption of all the terms which had been agreed upon with the American Board, by the Commissioners of the United Foreign Missionary Society, when a transfer was to be made of the concerns and property of the latter Board to the former. In this attempt, it has been seen, they failed. The attempt, however, was renewed in 1831; when a Committee of conference with the American Board was appointed, with direction to report to the General Assembly of the following year (1832). This report was made accordingly, and contained a long and elaborate statement, setting forth the many reasons and considerations, which should induce the General Assembly, as the representative of the Presbyterian denomination, to enter into a formal agreement to co-operate with the American Board, without attempting any other organization for the prosecution of Foreign Missions; and endeavoring to obviate the objections which might be urged against such a measure. The writer was present when this report was read, and it commanded all his attention. Not being able to obtain an inspection of the report, he has been obliged to make the statement of its purport from memory. In preparing most of the statements of this sketch, he has had his authorities before him; and has felt regret whenever it has been otherwise. But the Assembly again acted as they had done in 1826. The short minute adopted on the subject is as follows:

"Thursday morning, May 31.—The report was taken up, and, after some discussion, the following resolution was adopted, viz.:

"*Resolved*, That while the Assembly would express no opinion in relation to the principles contained in the report, they cordially recommend the American Board of Commissioners for Foreign Missions to the affection and patronage of their churches."

Thus it appears that till 1836, there was never a General Assembly in which the friends of a formal union of the Presbyterian Church with the American Board had influence enough to obtain an act of the supreme judicatory, in favor of such a measure. Nor indeed was such a measure formally adopted by the Assembly of 1836; although what was actually done, was calculated, and probably intended, to make the Presbyterian Church entirely subservient, in its missionary concerns, to that Board.

Of the three classes of Presbyterians that have been mentioned, the two latter, it appears, co-operated cheerfully and liberally with the American Board, during the period in which there was no missionary organization in the Church of which they were members. To this co-operation, a portion of the efficiency and extensive success of the American Board ought, in justice, to be attributed. Its amount it would be difficult to calculate, and the plan of this sketch does not require that an estimate should be attempted. The praise of all success belongs to God alone, whatever instrumentality He may use and honor in its production. The present writer has always commended the wisdom generally displayed, in the plans and operations of that Board, and the zeal and indefatigable perseverance with which they have been executed. Till the formation of the Western Board of Foreign Missions, his mite of influence and pecuniary contribution was given to it; and he has never ceased to pray for its success, and to rejoice in its usefulness and prosperity.

THEORY OF "CHURCH" MISSIONS. [The New Testament contains frequent references to the missionary labors of the early Christians. It was a work commanded by our Lord Himself. It was to be begun at home, "at Jerusalem." It was to be continued "among all nations" (Luke xxiv. 47). The Acts of the Apostles is chiefly a record of these labors. From the inspired narrative, we learn that the work of missions was regarded as the common work of the Church, a work in which all its members, clerical and lay, men and women, were called to take an active part. This was done by them all, each in his own sphere, yet under some simple form of organization. This organization, we may believe, was that of the Church itself (Acts xi. 22, xiii. 1–4, xiv. 27, xv. 22, etc.). Hence we reasonably infer that the work of sending the Gospel to the unevangelized is the proper work of the Church as such; and we understand the last commandment of our Lord, Matt. xxviii. 19, 20, as teaching this doctrine. It is a commandment which is obligatory on all the disciples of Christ, upon each in his place, but which cannot be fully obeyed by Christians apart from the Church; the recognition and due ordering of men's right to preach and to administer the sacraments, duties expressly mentioned in this commandment, are matters which nearly all Christians consider as of Church authority. This authority is to be exercised, not to hinder or fetter, but to foster, direct, and promote the great object of making disciples of all nations. In this we see one of the noblest purposes of the Church; and the form of church government, and much more the doctrines embraced, which best engage the disciples of Christ in the work of missions, and best promote their usefulness in this work, may well be considered as most in accordance with the divine standard. In these views also we see the duty of all Christian people—of ministers and other church officers especially—to enter fully on the work of evangelization, not waiting for nor relying on external or "Voluntary" agency to take this duty from their hands, but themselves fulfilling it as pertaining to their office and place in the Church of Christ equally with any other part of their sacred duties; and the duty of all the members of the Church, to live for no object inferior to the glory of Christ in the conversion of the world.

It is easy to frame the missionary plans of the Church in agreement with this theory. The work of missions is indeed great. It embraces all the unevangelized nations. It includes every good method of planting and building up the Church. Its object is simple, and the means it employs to achieve this object are varied, according to the various gifts of the laborers, and the differing circumstances of unevangelized people. It is not intended, however, to describe here at any length the nature of this work. While its general object is well understood, the means of promoting this object are equally plain; they are very much the same as are employed in our churches in this country: the preaching of the Gospel; education of children and youth under Christian influence in schools of different kinds; translation and printing of the Holy Scriptures, and the preparation of other Christian books; forming of churches, Presbyteries, and Synods. All of these means look to the end of the conversion of souls, or the spread and reception of the religion of the Lord Jesus Christ as the great salvation.

As these divinely appointed means are attended with success, the work of missions will pass more and more into the hands of native ministers of the Gospel supported by native churches, until eventually the work of the foreign missionary will come to a happy end. In the meantime, all his plans and measures should be directed to this object, and the utmost care should be taken in the training, employment, and support of native missionary laborers, in the building of churches, etc., that precedents should not be established which, by their pecuniary cost, or by reason of any foreign peculiarities, would prove embarrassing to the growth and self-support of the native Church. The main thing to be kept in view by the foreign missionary is that of teaching the great truths of the Gospel, clearly and fully, exemplifying these lessons in his life, and depending on the influences of the Holy Spirit, sought constantly in prayer, to apply unto men the benefits of redemption.

The followers of Christ are living in different countries. A universal missionary institution could be conducted only on the plan of concentrating the whole power in the hands of a few men, who would be virtually irresponsible to their brethren. The fallen Church of Rome is the only body of professed Christians that attempts to carry forward missions by such an organization, and her success does not invite imitation. Even when Evangelical Christians living in the same country, though delightfully one in spirit and in purpose, adopt different views of doctrinal and ecclesiastical questions. Their harmony and efficiency at home would not be promoted by their fusion into one denomination, neither would their missionary labors abroad be more effective by being placed under the charge of a common Society. Questions about the mode and subjects of baptism, the use of ruling elders in the Church, the ordination of ministers, the exercise of church discipline, not to instance purely doctrinal points, present themselves as readily at a missionary station, when the Gospel begins to bring forth fruit in the conversion of souls, as they do in a Christian land; and if the missionaries hold conflicting opinions on these questions, the peace and prosperity of their infant churches are likely to be seriously injured.

It is best for each large body of Christians to have its own missionary organization; and the simpler this can be made the better. Its form must depend in some degree on the distinctive institutions and customs of the denomination: the prevailing views of church government in each body will materially influence the form of missionary movement. On the Independent theory, which considers every particular church as sustaining no relations to other churches, excepting those of Christian fellowship, it would be difficult, yet not impracticable, to frame a Missionary Society on a plan that would secure direct responsibility to the churches as churches. As commonly understood this form of church government provides no common court of appeal, nor any general superintending body with authoritative power. Recourse is usually had to some kind of associated action separate from the churches, or not ecclesiastical; and reliance is placed mainly on the public opinion of the denomination for a satisfactory administration of its affairs. The Methodist, Episcopal, and Presbyterian denominations have their respective peculiarities, also, and it would be easy to show how these must influence the question of missionary polity. But the principle of Representation admits of many applications. In religious institutions, however, it ought seldom if ever to rest on a pecuniary basis.

A Society may be denominational, and yet not ecclesiastical,—supported exclusively by the members of some one denomination, sending forth only missionaries of its order, and yet not amenable to its ecclesiastical authorities, but to those persons only who contribute to its funds, or who are associated in a certain way. In some conditions of the Church, this form may be expedient, and for a time the only one practicable; as where the prevailing state of feeling is hostile to missions. In the Presbyterian Church, it should be acknowledged with gratitude, no expedient of this kind is needful. The duty of Christian missions is commonly recognized, and it is quite practicable to frame a missionary organization amenable to its Church courts, and at the same time open to the healthful influence of public opinion. In this way the opportunity is offered to all its members to promote the missionary work, with the same free choice in action, the same safeguards of truth and order, the same responsibility to ecclesiastical supervision, the same power resulting from oneness of views, purity of doctrine, and the indwelling of the Spirit of Christ, the spirit of missions,—precisely the same abroad, as at home; in the Presbytery of Lodiana as in the Presbytery of New York.—"Foreign Missions," 1868.]

THE WESTERN FOREIGN MISSIONARY SOCIETY.

IN the month of November, 1831, the Synod of Pittsburgh—always the most forward and active Synod of the Presbyterian Church in missionary enterprise and effort—formed the Western Foreign Missionary Society. The origin, and the general nature and design of this institution, may be learned from the following extracts from the Circular letter, issued immediately after its formation, and from the first four articles of its Constitution. Having declared that the Society "did not originate in any feeling of jealousy or dissatisfaction with the American Board of Commissioners for Foreign Missions—in any desire to diminish its resources or impair that measure of public confidence which it certainly and justly enjoys," the Circular proceeds as follows:

"As there is much diversity and fluctuation of opinion in the General Assemblies of our Church, as to the propriety of undertaking Foreign Missions at all, or in union with Domestic, it is conceived that no existing Board does, in fact, fill that place which is here proposed, and which seems requisite to a complete enlistment of the charities and prayers of the whole Presbyterian Church, in the great and glorious work of Missions to the heathen. The practice of designating those who are to watch over her interests, and dispense her charities through her regularly constituted judicatories, has so long existed in the Presbyterian Church, and is so interwoven with her form of government, that its absence from such stated plans of evangelical effort as the Missionary cause presents, does very naturally produce dissatisfaction and lukewarmness in some, and an almost entire neglect of the great object in others. Such, accordingly, has been the fact, to a great extent, in the Middle and Western States, and nothing but a plan which recognizes the Church, in her very organization, as a society for Missions to the heathen, and which presents such a kind of Presbyterial representation and supervision as gives an ecclesiastical responsibility to her agents, can, it is believed, ever fully bring up her Presbyteries and churches 'to the help of the Lord against the mighty.' The obvious want of such an arrangement, felt more deeply here than in some other parts of the Presbyterian Church, led the Synod of Pittsburgh at its late sessions to move in this business; partly from the belief that, under existing circumstances, it would be better for some Synod which could be nearly or quite harmonious in its measures, to undertake the plan, than for the General Assembly to attempt it; and partly from the conviction that a central location would better suit distant parts of the country, and that this, near one of the theological seminaries of the Church, and yet unembarked actively in any great public enterprise, would, at least for a time, answer a better purpose, especially for Western Missions, than any other. Aside from such a degree of Synodical supervision as seemed necessary to the very existence of such a society, you will see by examining the accompanying constitution, that it is strictly a Presbyterial arrangement, and gives the management of the whole concern to those from whom the resources are to be drawn. It aims at uniting those portions of the Presbyterian Church which prefer such a plan of operation, in a new, earnest, and persevering endeavor, to fulfill the duty which we owe to the heathen of our own and foreign lands; and of imparting to our church judicatories as such, a due sense of responsibility, and such a missionary impulse as these eventful times imperiously require. If the undertaking, owned and blessed of God, meets the friendly consideration of our churches and Presbyteries, it will be subject to their control, and can, if they wish it, be transferred, as to the centre of its operations, to whatever part of the Church they please. In the meantime, dear brother, let us be up and doing. We are anxious to despatch, if possible, this very year, a mission to Central Africa, or some still more eligible unoccupied field on the Eastern continent; and we would be glad at the same time to institute a Western mission, so soon as we may be able to make a judicious selection of the best opening for such an effort."

CONSTITUTION. "Article 1. This Society shall be composed of the Ministers, Sessions, and Churches of the Synod of Pittsburgh, together with those of any other Synod or Synods, Presbytery or Presbyteries, that may hereafter formally unite with them, and shall be known by the name of the Western Foreign Missionary Society of the United States.

"2. The objects of the Society shall be to aid in fulfilling the last great command of the glorified Redeemer, by conveying the Gospel to whatever parts of the Heathen and antichristian world the providence of God may enable this Society to extend its evangelical exertions.

"3. The centre of its operations shall be the city of Pittsburgh, at least until such times as the Board of Directors shall judge that the interests of the cause require a change of location, which, however, shall never be effected without the consent of the Synod of Pittsburgh; and in the event of such a change, then the special provisions of a Synodical supervision and representation, mentioned in this constitution, shall be transferred to the General Assembly, or to that particular Synod within whose bounds the operations of the Society shall be concentred.

"4. The general superintendence of the interests of this Society shall be confided to a Board of Directors, to be appointed in the following manner, to wit: The Synod shall elect, at the present time, of persons residing in Pittsburgh and its vicinity, six Ministers and six Ruling Elders, whose terms of service shall be so arranged that those of two Ministers and two Ruling Elders shall expire at the end of one year, and two of each at the end of two years, and the remaining two at the end of three years, and the Synod shall ever after elect annually one-third of this number, or two Ministers and two Ruling Elders; and in the event of a renewal of the charter of the Western Missionary Society, so amended as to meet the present objects of this Society, then the said twelve persons herein mentioned shall constitute, for the time being, the trustees and legal representatives of the Synod; to fulfill the duties of such trust in the manner which may be specified in the said charter. 2. The Synod shall also elect one Minister and one Ruling Elder, from each of the Presbyteries now composing this body, the one-half, or four Ministers and four Elders, to be chosen for two years, and the remaining four for one year, but after the expiration of the term of service for which they shall be severally chosen, this election shall devolve upon the Presbyteries respectively; and the same right shall be extended to any Presbytery or Presbyteries, which may hereafter be formed within its bounds. 3. And whenever any Presbytery or Presbyteries belonging to other Synod or Synods, shall become regularly united with this Society, by vote and actual contribution to its funds, every such Presbytery shall be entitled, in like manner, to the right of appointing one Minister and one Ruling Elder, to serve for the term of two years, leaving it to the Board of Directors so to fix the two classes as that the change for each and every year shall be as nearly as possible equal to the others; and these persons so appointed shall constitute a Board, to be styled the Board of Directors of the Western Foreign Missionary Society, and the said Board shall meet annually in the city of Pittsburgh, on the Tuesday preceding the second Thursday in May, at 3 o'clock P.M. and oftener on the call of the President, at the request of the Executive Committee, or on that of any three other members of the Board. The election of the Board of Directors shall be made by ballot, and in reference to those to be chosen by the Synod, the rule shall be, after the first election, to make a nomination at least one day previous to that on which the choice is to be made."

The remaining four articles of the Constitution relate to the details of the Society—the choice of a President, of a Vice-President, of honorary Vice-Presidents and honorary Directors, of a Corresponding and Recording Secretary, of a Treasurer, and an Executive Committee, and the prescription of the duties of these officers and agents severally.

The Society, when first organized by the Synod, consisted of twenty-eight directors; and they immediately chose a President, Vice-President, an Executive Committee, consisting of five clergymen and four laymen, with a Corresponding Secretary and Treasurer. The Board also, agreeably to an authority granted in the

Constitution, elected at the first meeting fifteen honorary Vice-Presidents and thirteen honorary Directors.

It is due to the Rev. Elisha P. Swift, the first Corresponding Secretary of this Society, to state, that its origin is to be traced, principally, to his ardent zeal in the missionary cause, and to his views of the importance of an institution organized in the manner exhibited in the foregoing documents. He submitted his ideas to his brethren of the Synod, by whom, after due deliberation, they were adopted. He drafted the Constitution and wrote the circular letter, and on him, under the direction and cheerful co-operation of the Executive Committee, rested the principal burden of labor and effort in carrying into effect the plan of the Society. He resigned for this purpose the pastoral charge of a congregation, between whom and himself a strong and tender attachment existed; and devoted all his time and faculties to give activity and efficiency to the infant institution. Destitute of funds, it threatened for a short period to languish; but it soon received a quickening impulse from the liberal donation of a thousand dollars from the Hon. Walter Lowrie, the Secretary of the Senate of the United States. This gift was made in a manner which, for a considerable time, left the donor unknown. It equalled in amount the annual salary of the Corresponding Secretary, and was appropriated by the donor to that object; thus freeing him from all imputation of seeking emolument for himself, while he earnestly solicited pecuniary contributions to the funds of the Society.

EXECUTIVE OFFICERS. [The Rev. Elisha P. Swift, D.D., was born in Williamstown, Mass., August 12, 1792. He graduated at Williams College in September, 1813, and at Princeton Theological Seminary, after a full course, in September, 1816. He was ordained as a foreign missionary in connection with the American Board in 1817; but reasons of health in the family prevented his going to a foreign field. He spent some months, however, on visits to churches to promote the missionary cause in what was then the Western country. After supplying a church in Delaware for a year, he accepted a call to the Second Presbyterian church, Pittsburgh, Pa., where his ministry was greatly prospered. He continued in this charge from 1819 to March, 1833. His was a ministry of success and power. He was endeared to his church as a pastor, yet his pulpit was his throne.

Soon after his accepting the call of this church, and while he was its pastor, he was appointed as a member of the Synod's Missionary Board of Trust, or Executive Committee as it would now be called. In its service he was for some years an unsalaried secretary, until the Board was merged in the General Assembly's Board of Domestic Missions. During these years he no doubt became well acquainted with the principles and methods of the work of missions, Foreign and Domestic, which had been adopted for many years in the two Synods of Virginia and Pittsburgh. Their views were generally held in that part of the Presbyterian Church, and especially in the latter Synod. And when the time came for organizing a Foreign Missionary Society, the movement for this purpose was made with entire harmony after counsel with many leading ministers and elders. In other parts of this volume particular information is given as to this important movement. Our reference to it here is for two reasons—one general, the other personal. In general, a comparison shows that the principles and methods of the older societies and of the new one are identical, with only minor changes adapting the new society to its special work. Personally, all felt as did the writer of these lines, that it was a privilege to hear the noble speech of Dr. Swift, when this subject was under consideration by the Synod. By a unanimous vote it was resolved to enter upon this work for Christ our Lord, relying on His Providence and Grace.

At the request of his brethren generally, no less than by the vote of the Board, Dr. Swift was constrained to accept the appointment of Corresponding Secretary of the new Society; his church very reluctantly accepted his resignation. With what ability and success he fulfilled the arduous duties of this office, it were needless to relate. At some disadvantage from the want of early business experience, he yet fulfilled the arduous duties of this office with very great success. In office work; in meetings of the Committee and the Directors; in interviews with friends of the cause, with missionaries going forth and with persons looking to missionary life; in correspondence largely with missionaries in the field on varied and often difficult subjects; in studying missionary countries and people, and their various religions; in visits at farewell and often at distant meetings, and many preaching services in churches near and far; in editing the *Missionary Chronicle* and other publications, and preparing the Annual Reports to May, 1836, inclusive; in being present at Presbyteries, Synods, and the General Assembly,—in such duties as these, weary days and often late hours at night were passed, and the tender relations of domestic life—of parents and young children—were often embarrassed. Yet it was a blessed service in such a cause, for such Christian brethren, for such a Saviour!

There came another call, however, to a new church in Alleghany, which had among its members former parishioners and friends. Earnest consultations with his co-laborers in the Board followed. The leadings of

Providence and of the Holy Spirit were carefully studied. At last the way of duty seemed to be plain. The secretaryship was to be resigned when it seemed probable that a successor could be obtained, who would be welcomed by the Church. The call to the church was accepted October 9, 1835, but the duties of the missionary office were continued until January, 1836. The charge of the church was held, with ever affectionate relations, until his lamented death, April 3, 1865.

The Annual Report of the Board of Foreign Missions to the General Assembly of 1865, contains a sympathetic record of the death of Drs. William W. Phillips, George Potts, and Elisha P. Swift, members of the Board. The *Foreign Missionary*, of May, 1865, also refers to these eminent ministers as having entered into rest. Its concluding record of Dr. Swift by the writer of this Note is here reprinted:

"To the end of his life Dr. Swift was a most faithful friend of this cause of missions. Often his eloquent voice pleaded for its interests with his Christian brethren, and it is known that it was daily aided by his prayers, in his private devotions, with special particularity. In our last interview with him, several months before his departure, information was given as to a certain matter in one of our eastern missions—information which we had reason to know was intended to be made use of in the closet and not in any public way. It was true of both our revered and beloved friends, Dr. Phillips and Dr. Swift, [the former, pastor of the First Presbyterian church, New York, and President of the Board of Foreign Missions from 1837 until his lamented death in 1865], that their prayers for the cause of missions were remarkable—excelling in breadth, in proper specification, in fervor; they were never omitted in the services of the sanctuary, and their impressiveness could easily be ascribed in part to the habitual intercessions of their private hours. Our cause has suffered a great loss in the removal of these men of prayer. Eminent as they were in talents and in position, they were not less eminent in prayer. May their mantle fall on their brethren!"]

[On a former page a brief Note was inserted concerning the Rev. E. McCurdy, D.D., for many years voluntary Treasurer of the Pittsburgh Synodical Missions, and one of its most efficient Directors. It would seem suitable to insert also a Note concerning another of the Executive officers to whom the Society was greatly indebted for efficient support, the Rev. Francis Herron, D.D., Pastor of the First Presbyterian church, Pittsburgh.

It was understood that he felt at first some hesitation as to the expediency of organizing the Society at that time, when the current expenses and the endowment of the Western Theological Seminary pressed so heavily on the churches of the Synod of Pittsburgh, and especially on the church under his pastoral charge. But he would not discourage his brethren, much less oppose so great a work as this new movement for sending the Gospel to the heathen, a cause with which he was in the fullest sympathy; and both he and his influential congregation were most efficient friends of the Society. He was usually Chairman of its Executive Committee, as he had been also of its Board of Trust in many former years. A leading member of his church, the Hon. Harmer Denny, a member of Congress, was the first President of the Society.

Dr. Herron was born near Carlisle, Pa., June 28, 1771; graduated at Dickinson College, 1794; ordained as Pastor of Rocky Spring church, Pa., April 9, 1800; and after a happy and prospered ministry there, he accepted a call to the First Church of Pittsburgh, Pa., June, 1811. This church was then small in the number of its members, in debt, and greatly discouraged. A low tone of spiritual life characterized many of its members, so that not even a prayer-meeting was held; and the young pastor had to establish a meeting against the opposition of some members of the church. Pittsburgh was then but a small place. The church property was soon afterwards sold by the sheriff; it was bought by the pastor, a part of its land sold by him, efficient management maintained, and the property restored to the church. Under his efficient ministry, with the divine blessing, this church became one of the largest and strongest in our denomination long before its noble minister resigned its charge; and so it is to this day.

Becoming infirm, he resigned his church in 1849, but lived revered among his people until his death, December 6, 1860, in the 81st year of his age, greatly mourned over by all classes in the now large city, and by the Church at large. He was a large, manly-looking man, and he was as genial and good as he looked; a pillar of strength for every good cause, and greatly blessed in his ministry. The writer of these Notes gladly pays this tribute to his memory, based on personal knowledge gained in college and seminary days, and the acquaintance afterwards of many years. It would be a real pleasure also to refer in like manner to other Western Pennsylvania clergymen and laymen, such as Drs. McMillan, Brown, Elliott, Jennings, Beatty, Weed, Stockton, Patterson, Fairchild, Messrs. Tait, McPherrin, Hughes, Johnston, Baird, and others not a few: besides many like-minded, noble men, in other parts of the country, who were men consecrated to Christ, earnest friends of missions and of every good work, and steadfast in the faith; but the limits prescribed to these pages do not admit of these tributes. Blessed is the memory of such men!]

FIRST YEAR OF THE SOCIETY'S WORK.
A few extracts from the life of the Rev. Joseph W. Barr, by the Corresponding Secretary of the Society, published in March, 1833, will give a general view of the operations of the Society during the first year of its existence. After a narrative of the proceedings of the Synod of Pittsburgh in the organization of the Society, the Secretary says:

"The Board of Directors then appointed, constituted immediately after the rising of Synod, and chose an Executive Committee, by which regular monthly meetings have been ever since held. The committee, in their first circular, expressed the determination to undertake the establishment of a mission in Western Africa, as soon as circumstances would permit; and the subject was laid before Societies of Inquiry on Missions, in the Theological Seminaries of Princeton and Alleghanytown. Communications were soon after received from Mr. John B. Pinney, of the Theological Seminary at Princeton, and Messrs. John C. Lowrie and William Reed, of the Western Theological Seminary, offering to place themselves under the care and direction of the Executive Committee, as missionaries to the Heathen. . . . . During the summer, Mr. Pinney, whose mind had been strongly inclined to an African mission, became anxious to have an early period designated, at which the undertaking might be expected to commence; and on being apprised that this would be done as soon as a suitable fellow-laborer could be provided for that field, he submitted the solemn question to the consideration of one who was known to have devoted himself to the work, and who possessed peculiar qualifications for such an undertaking; this person was Mr. Joseph W. Barr."

"The present state of this infant Society, to which a number of Presbyteries, besides those originally included, have given the promise of their efficient co-operation during the past year, may be, in part, learned from the subjoined statement of its missionary arrangements:

MISSIONS OF THE SOCIETY. "Since its organization, the Board has received under its care, seven missionaries, besides two or three assistants, intended for the Western mission. These have been distributed in the following manner:

"1. To Western Africa, two. Rev. Messrs. John B. Pinney and Joseph W. Barr.

"2. To Northern India, three. Messrs. John C. Lowrie and William Reed, two of these brethren, are expected to sail from this country for Calcutta about the 1st of May.

"3. To the Indians west of the Mississippi, two. One of these brethren is expected to proceed, in company with some other person, during the ensuing summer, to the site of the proposed establishment, and make preparations for the reception of the other members in the following autumn.

"To Western and eventually Central Africa, this Society has from the beginning looked, as one of the principal fields of its intended operations. To that benighted land it consecrated its first efforts: and all the information which has been since received, has but tended to increase its desire to draw, in a special manner, the attention of American Christians, and of young men devoted to the cause of missions, to that long neglected and interesting part of the globe."

Keeping in view the compendious nature of this work, the several missions of the Society now in contemplation will be noticed in the order in which they were sent out; and the history of each will be continuously sketched till the first meeting of the Board in October, 1837.

MISSION TO WESTERN AFRICA. From the above quotation it appears that Central Africa was contemplated, as ultimately the principal field in which this mission was expected to operate; and where probably its chief seat would be located. In order to this, however, it was necessary that the Society should have an establishment on the western coast, to which its supplies might be sent, by which a communication might be kept up with the Society at home, and where the missionaries destined to the interior might reside till their acclimation should have taken place. Such were the original views of the Society; views which are not yet relinquished, notwithstanding the severe trials with which God, in His holy sovereignty, has seen meet hitherto to exercise the faith, patience, and perseverance of His people.

Messrs. John B. Pinney and Joseph W. Barr were, as already stated, the first missionaries designated to Africa. They were both from the Theological Seminary at Princeton, and both made a voluntary offer of themselves for this hazardous mission. They were ordained together October 12, 1832, by the Presbytery of Philadelphia, specially called for the purpose. Their beloved professors, Drs. Alexander and Miller, by invitation of the Presbytery, took the principal parts of the ordination service, which was numerously attended in the Sixth Presbyterian church, and pervaded by a deep solemnity. The vessel in which they were to go to Liberia was to sail from Norfolk in Virginia about the close of the current month. Thither, therefore, a few days after their ordination, they hastily repaired, having taken a most solemn and affecting farewell of their Philadelphia friends in a public meeting called for the purpose. They arrived in Norfolk on the 23d of October, and found that the vessel in which their passage was taken would not sail till the 5th of the following month. In the intervening days, with a view to promote the interests of the mission, Mr. Barr visited Richmond and Petersburgh. Having made arrangements in the latter place for a public missionary meeting, to be attended by himself on Tuesday, he returned to preach at Richmond on the preceding Sabbath. But the time had arrived at which he was to preach no more. A friend who was with him in his last hours, wrote and published an interesting account of his death, from which our limits will permit us to give only the following extracts:

"At nine o'clock on Saturday night, he was apparently in perfect health. We passed the evening with him, in company with a few friends of missions, who felt deeply interested in the enterprise on which he was about to embark. He was slightly indisposed, as he afterwards stated, when he retired to his chamber for the night. About one o'clock he was taken violently ill of cholera. Able physicians were immediately called in, and the usual remedies administered; but in vain—his Lord and Master had called for him. The progress of his disease was so rapid as to baffle the efforts of medical skill—and at three o'clock on Sabbath afternoon he was released from his sufferings, and admitted, we trust, into the rest which the Lord has prepared for His people.

"It will be consolatory to his distant friends, and to the young ministers who were recently his fellow students, to know that he appeared to be perfectly resigned to this mysterious stroke of Providence. Though his heart, filled with compassion for the perishing, was fixed on the work of missions in Africa, to which he had dedicated his life—yet he was willing to leave it and to die. He discovered no alarm at the approach and near prospect of death. The summons, though sudden and unexpected, did not find him unprepared. On being asked by the writer concerning the state of his mind, he expressed with earnestness his confidence in God and submission to His will, adding: 'the blood of Christ cleanseth from all sin.' Here rested his hope, on the Rock of Ages—and it sustained him in the hour of trial. He repeatedly expressed the same unshaken trust in the Lord, to other Christian brethren, who attended him during his short illness. Death to him was a vanquished enemy. In the near view of eternity he could pray in the language of the apostle, 'Even so, come, Lord Jesus.' "

Mr. Barr was a youth of great promise, and seldom has a death been more lamented than his. It left his beloved missionary brother, Mr. Pinney, without a companion for the African Mission, and rendered it questionable whether it were expedient, or even lawful, for him to go alone on the perilous enterprise in which both had embarked. But having waited till the month of January following, without any one offering to accompany him, and all his arrangements for departure being made, his zeal in the cause in which he had engaged determined him to embrace an opportunity which offered, and to sail for Liberia—in hope that his unaided efforts might prove an encouragement and prepare the way for others to follow him. After a prosperous voyage he arrived at Monrovia on the 16th of February, 1833. He remained in Africa about four months; and during this period he made an exploring excursion into the interior, as far as a native prince, through whose country he had to pass, would permit him to proceed. At the commencement of the rainy season, he found that his necessary inactivity in Africa during its continuance, would be more expensive than a voyage home; where he might be active in preaching, and in endeavoring to obtain associates in his missionary labors. He arrived in Philadelphia in the month of July, and his motives for return were approved by the Executive Committee of the Board. By information received from him, the Committee were enabled to select two stations, whose relative situations, both as to the colony and the interior nations, would afford great facility for disseminating the Gospel in Africa.

A few days before the arrival of Mr. Pinney, Messrs. John Cloud and Matthew Laird, who had been previously received under the care of the Board, as candidates for the missionary service, were designated as a reinforcement to the African Mission. After spending some time in visiting the churches, these missionaries, together with Mrs. Laird and Mr. James Temple, a young man of color under the care of the Presbytery of Philadelphia, and who had been received as an assistant, were regularly organized as a missionary body in New York in October; and sailed from Norfolk for Liberia on the 6th of November following. About the same time, missionaries from two other societies in our country, were appointed to repair to the western coast of that benighted continent. Mr. Pinney, shortly before his embarkation with the other missionaries, received from the Board of Managers of the American Colonization Society, the appointment of temporary Agent and Governor of Liberia; and after consulting with the Corresponding Secretary and other friends of the Society, it was judged best that he should consent to act in that capacity, till a permanent agent could be obtained. He accordingly performed the duties of colonial agent for a time, expressing his earnest hope that other arrangements might soon be made by the Colonization Society.

The ship *Jupiter*, in which the missionaries embarked, arrived at Monrovia on the 31st of December (1833), after a passage of fifty-six days. The missionaries were enabled, soon after their arrival, to rent a suitable tenement for their accommodation, during their stay in Monrovia, and all the members of the mission soon experienced, in succession, the attacks of the African fever. In most instances, the fever in the past winter had been uncommonly mild, and much fewer cases of mortality had occurred among the emigrants than in former years; from which it was hoped that the missionaries, most of whom had experienced more than one return of the disease, would have little to fear from any future attack. But these cheering prospects of a safe and easy acclimation, and the expectation of an uncommonly healthy season in the colony, were but the precursors of a mortality which thinned the ranks of the emigrants, while it almost entirely extinguished the hope of the two important missions which had lately arrived.

Mr. Cloud, unwilling to lose time by unnecessary delay, and anxious to ascertain the prospects at Cape Mount, a place one hundred and fifty miles up the coast, before the arrangements of the mission were finally made, resolved (too soon it would appear after his recovery) to embrace an opportunity then offering, to embark on board a vessel going up the coast. The heat of the weather—the detention of the coaster by adverse winds—an incautious exposure to night air, and the yet debilitated state of his health, brought on an early relapse, which, in the absence of needful medicines, of even a tolerably comfortable place in sickness, or a kind friend to attend him, soon prepared the way for cholera morbus, and the transition of this to a malignant dysentery. When the vessel returned to Monrovia, on the 8th of April, after an absence of ten days, he was found unable to walk or stand, and his physician soon after pronounced it impossible to arrest his malady. During the few days of his survival, Mr. and Mrs. Laird, with a kindness and solicitude which nothing could surpass, waited night and day around the bed of their beloved associate; and he had no sooner expired than it was found that the fatal malady had transferred itself with undiminished violence to them. Mr. Laird was first attacked, and his wife, though a woman of no ordinary faith and fortitude, sunk before the prospect of another victim, so soon to be made in the person of her husband. She expired on the 3d of May; and on the day following, her husband closed his eyes in death.

When it was known among the native tribes around Monrovia, that the voice of those kind and devoted friends, who had come to them with the words of eternal life, was to be heard no more, they are said to have exhibited a regret as solemn and striking as it appeared to be sincere; and who, that considers how often the light of hope for this unfortunate people has but reached the shores of Africa, and then died away, can avoid a heartfelt sympathy in these touching expressions of a conscious bereavement? Of these three courageous and devoted servants of Christ, this is not the place to speak at large. All that can be added is, that they carried with them from their native shores the esteem of all who knew them, and entered upon their perilous undertaking with great apparent desire to live and suffer for the good of the heathen; and that they met the early and beclouded end of their enterprise, in the possession of a calm and cheerful anticipation of immortal felicity.

Soon after the decease of Mr. Laird, Mr. Temple withdrew from the mission and returned to the United States; while Mr. Pinney, temporarily fulfilling the duties of Colonial Agent, and still resolving to resume and prosecute the missionary work, remained at his post amidst the most appalling scenes of dispersion and death, among those who had accompanied him on his return to Africa. After having conferred important good upon the colony by the judicious fulfilment of the duties of Colonial Agent, he retired from that office and resumed his missionary labors. In the September following, he was joined by Mr. J. F. C. Finley, who had repaired to Liberia to become a superintendent and teacher of native schools; and they soon after proceeded to erect a comfortable mission-house at Millsburgh, and open a small farm for the use of the mission—on which a supply of coffee, lime, grove, and orange trees, and also of cassada, sweet potatoes, plantain, and banana were planted. Shortly after, however, these two brethren, exhausted by disease, and no longer able to prosecute their labors, embarked for the United States; having suspended all further efforts for the present, and left the mission premises and property in Millsburgh, in trust, with the Baptist missionaries, by whom the house has since been occupied.

From the departure from Africa of Messrs. Pinney and Finley, in an early part of the summer of 1835, till the month of December following, the Western Foreign Missionary Society was destitute of a single African missionary. Mr. Pinney, indeed, was still living, and still expressing his willingness, should his life be spared and his health restored, to return to the field of his painful and hazardous labors. But his constitution was so shattered that his ultimate restoration, to such a degree of firmness as to warrant the resumption of his former situation, was exceedingly problematical; and it may here be added, that although his health is considerably improved, it is still questionable whether he ought ever again to risk an exposure to a climate which repeated trials have demonstrated that he cannot encounter, without the most imminent peril of his life and usefulness.

In the autumn of 1835, Mr. Ephraim Titler, a colored man, who had resided for some time in Liberia, and who, with his wife, had been employed, under the auspices of Mr. Pinney, in teaching a school of native Africans near the Junk River, was received as a missionary by the Western Board. He had previously spent nearly a year in the United States, employing as much time as he could command in acquiring the knowledge which might qualify him to receive license to preach the Gospel. He was licensed by the Presbytery of Philadelphia, with an express reference to his return as a missionary to Africa, in the month of September, 1836. He sailed from Wilmington, North Carolina, on the 31st of December following, in a vessel chartered by the American Colonization Society, with a number of emigrants to Liberia, and arrived in safety at Monrovia in the following February. He was instructed to commence his labors at Boblee, a station selected by Mr. Pinney as having every facility of access to the natives, and owing to its elevated situation, affording the best prospect of health. He has located himself at that place, agreeably to his instructions, and according to communications received from him, with fair prospects of success.

In closing the gloomy account of this African Mission, it is believed that particular attention is due to what is said on the subject in the fifth and last report of the Western Foreign Missionary Society, made in May, 1837. It is as follows:

"It is the intention of the Executive Committee, as fast as they can procure suitable and educated colored men, to strengthen and enlarge this mission. The employment of colored men, for building up the Redeemer's kingdom in Africa, the Committee now believe, has not been sufficiently attended to by the churches. Their own most painful experience, in the loss of their first missionaries; the lamentable loss of lives, among the missionaries of other societies, and particularly of that noble institution, the Church of England Missionary Society, whose persevering and untiring efforts in behalf of Western Africa exceed all others, have brought the subject of some other agency strongly before the Committee. Of their own missionaries sent to this field, but one survived, and he was forced to return in feeble health; and of the German Mission to Liberia, all died or returned. The number of missionaries and teachers sent to Sierra Leone by the Church of England Missionary Society, including chaplains sent by the government, from 1812 to 1830, was forty-four men and thirty-five women. The aggregate of time all these lived in that colony was 208 years; giving as an average two and one-half years to each; and more or less of that period was a time of severe sickness. A few returned home, but even then their labors were equally lost to the mission. The average of two and one-half years, as the life of a missionary, is a very painful subject of contemplation; but another view is even more so. Of these seventy-nine devoted men and women, five only lived from twelve to seventeen years—ten from five to eight years—thirteen from two to three years, and forty-four died the first year. How important for every Missionary Society to profit by such painful and distressing experience of their own and sister institutions.

"Now in the providence of God, an agency every way suited for the wants of Africa exists among us, and in the bosom of the Church. The constitution of the colored men of the Southern States has nothing to apprehend from the climate of Africa. If the friends of our Society at the South will select pious, suitable men, it will be the duty of the Committee to have them brought to the North, and see that they are properly educated. The result of this course, in a few years, would be a full supply of pious, educated, and qualified missionaries for this long discouraging field; and with the blessing of God, Africa 'redeemed, regenerated, and disenthralled,' would stretch forth her hand to Him. What Christian heart would not rejoice to see degraded, perishing, bleeding Africa, a nation scattered and peeled, for centuries the prey of the man-stealer and the murderer, rising from her long desolations, and rejoicing in the knowledge of redeeming love.

"No missionary society in the United States can bring this agency into action, with more advantages than the Foreign Missionary Society of the Presbyterian Church; and the Committee would most earnestly entreat their friends, and especially the pastors and elders of the churches, to assist them in carrying into efficient operation, the very important principles here suggested."

WEST CENTRAL AFRICA, VIA LIBERIA. [Preceding pages contain the views of the first Secretary of the Western Foreign Missionary Society, which show that the mission to Africa had as its chief field the central region of that dark land. Liberia seemed to be the door of entrance to this immense region and its vast population. Notwithstanding the distressing bereavements at first, the faith of the Church did not fail. The second Secretary called special attention to this mission, and particularly to the colored people of our own country, as eventually to furnish laborers for this interior field in the land of their forefathers. Both of these references to the African Mission were correct and of great moment. They have not yet been verified, to the degree then anticipated; but they will be, if the faith of the Church still fail not.

Two serious hindrances have stood in the way. One was and still is the extremely malarious coast region of the country, extending inland from fifty to a hundred miles, in which a large part of Liberia is situated. The Americo-Africans, mostly very poor, settled in this coast country, of which Monrovia is the chief town, and the capital of the Republic. The great discouragement of white men as missionaries, from which later experience shows that colored men have not been exempt though less liable thereto, has been the injurious climate. It proved to be fatal to devoted men and women after but short periods of service, or compelled them to withdraw from their work there, as already shown. They did not lose their reward, assuredly; the imperfect labors of missionaries in Liberia have not been in vain. Experience has led to greater care in not sending men ill adapted to the climate, and in their using proper precautions against its injurious influence. The existing Americo-Africans, now about 20,000, are in some degree acclimated; and among them are children and youths of both sexes, who greatly need better opportunities of training—not at all by sending them to America for this purpose, but by providing in their own land better means and opportunities of industrial education. This subject was referred to in the Annual Reports of the Board of Foreign Missions for 1890, page 12, and 1891, page 23.

The second hindrance to missionary labors in the interior, long insuperable, has to a large degree passed away. The border tribes, back of the coast, refused to allow foreigners to penetrate beyond their own boundaries. This was the case for many hundreds of miles along the west coast, even as far down as to the river Congo. But the time of exclusion from the interior of Africa is passing away, indeed is virtually at an end. As an example, Boporo, a considerable town and district, about a hundred miles inland from Monrovia, in an elevated and healthy country, is a place to which in former years missionaries could not be sent, but where they would now be welcomed. Indeed a missionary might have been stationed here several years ago, and the Board adopted measures to occupy this post. A talented, measurably well educated, colored man, then in the ranks as a missionary, was sent by the Board to Boporo. He was kindly received, and his report showed that the way was in a good degree prepared for missionary work. But his subsequent course made it plain that to some other laborer must be reserved the privilege of preaching the Gospel permanently in that place.

This Mission to Central Africa via Liberia must not be abandoned. It was the first begun, abroad, by our Church under its present system. It was sorely tried by early bereavements. Its conditions are now better understood. Its preliminary work has not been in vain. Its connection with the seven millions of Africo-Americans in our own country, and its influence on their religious and missionary destiny, must not be forgotten.

It may be of immeasurable importance to them. The Liberia Mission has been the most discouraging foreign work of our Church. Shall it not yet become one of the most blessed?]

MISSION TO NORTHERN INDIA. This mission was projected, as has been seen, at the very origin of the Western Foreign Missionary Society; and Messrs. John C. Lowrie and William Reed were the first missionaries that offered their services to the Society, and they were received under its care January 16, 1832. No preference for any field was stated by them; though the sending a mission to India or the East was then under the Society's consideration. The want of funds led to some delay, and they were engaged for several months after their licensure in visiting churches and meetings of Presbyteries and Synods for the cause of missions, one of them also spending several months at the Princeton Theological Seminary. The African Mission was sooner ready to be organized and sent forward to its field of operation.

In narrating the transactions relative to this and the remaining missions of the Western Foreign Missionary Society, the best general view may be presented, by abbreviating the authentic statements contained in the several annual reports of the Society itself. This plan will accordingly be pursued, with only such occasional departures from it as may be found indispensable. The following quotation is taken from the second Annual Report, read and adopted at the annual meeting, May 6, 1834:

"The last Annual Report stated, that the Rev. Messrs. William Reed and John C. Lowrie, with their wives, were expected to leave this country in a few weeks afterwards, to commence their contemplated mission in

Hindustan. Arrangements were made for their embarkation in the ship *Star*, of the port of Philadelphia, in May last. Never, it is believed, was the mind of the Christian public in that city, more deeply interested in the foreign missionary enterprise, than during the presence of the mission there, and the religious exercises which were connected with their final departure from it. The closing meeting will long be remembered by many, as well from the peculiar circumstances which tended to give effect to it, as from the divine influence which seemed to pervade it. . . . . This little band finally bid adieu to their native land, and the ship *Star* put to sea on the 30th of May, 1833, and arrived at Madeira on the 24th of June following. The temporary abode of the missionaries at that fertile and lovely spot in the ocean, tended not only to mitigate the fatigues of a long sea voyage, but somewhat to recruit the strength of Mrs. Lowrie, whose health had begun to be so far impaired, during the last few weeks of her residence in this country, as to threaten a confirmed pulmonary affection. The voyage was resumed on the 15th of July, and the *Star* arrived in the port of Calcutta on the 15th of October. The change of air incident to her passage into the southern hemisphere, and severe gales in doubling the Cape of Good Hope, appeared, the Committee regret to state, to confirm all the fears which had been entertained as to the character of Mrs. Lowrie's illness, and from that period she began gradually to become so feeble, that before the arrival of the *Star* in port, all hopes of her recovery were at an end.

"The missionaries were received at Calcutta with every mark of respect and affection, and to the Rev. William H. Pearce especially, will they and their friends in this country feel long and deeply indebted for the hospitality and kindness which were shown them. They were immediately taken into his family, and amidst the assiduous and affectionate attentions of Mr. and Mrs. Pearce and their friends, Mrs. Lowrie lingered until the 21st of November, when she expired; and from his hospitable mansion her mortal remains were borne to the house appointed for all living. To her deeply afflicted husband, thus early bereaved in a strange land, to the other two surviving members, to the Society and the cause of missions in India, the death of this amiable, intelligent, and devoted woman must be regarded as a very severe affliction. Her desires to devote herself to the spiritual good of the heathen were fervent, and her qualifications for the station were, to human view, uncommon; but He, for whose glory she left her native land, was pleased, doubtless for wise reasons, to disappoint her earthly hopes, and to require her associates, a few short weeks after their arrival, to consign her to the dust, there to proclaim, as she sleeps in Jesus on India's distant shores, the compassion of American Christians for its millions of degraded idolaters; and to invite others from her native land to come and prosecute the noble undertaking in which she fell.

"The Committee were led, from the information which they had previously obtained, to direct these brethren to seek some eligible position in the northern provinces of Hindustan as the field of their labors; but they were authorized to make a different selection if, on arriving in India and consulting with the friends of missions at Calcutta, it should be found expedient to do so."

[Other parts of the country were brought to their attention, particularly the district of Bundelkhund, not far south and west from Allahabad, containing a population of about three millions, and other millions in neighboring districts. The people are mostly Hindus, but not so much under the influence of the higher castes, " hard and fast," as in the northwest. They live not more than half as far from Calcutta as the people of the Punjab. Not much could be learned about them in those days, but their part of the country was said to be subject to fever and ague; now considered an erroneous impression. The reason for this Note is, that this district has not enjoyed more than transient visits of missionaries; it is still unoccupied territory, after so many years. The lately formed station of Jhansi is on its northern borders, accessible by railway.]

"After mature deliberation, and taking the advice of many judicious and well-informed counsellors, they came to the conclusion that the original designation of the Committee was decidedly the best, varying from it only in the selection of an adjoining province, somewhat further to the northwest, and inhabited by a people less bigoted in their attachment to Paganism. Besides this feature in the religious character of the people—their docility and desire to become acquainted with the English language—the comparative healthfulness of that part of India—its entire destitution of missionary instruction—and its proximity to, and commercial intercourse with, Afghanistan, Cashmere, and Thibet, extensive and populous regions as yet entirely unoccupied, are all considerations of importance, and going to show the propriety of the selection.

"Lodiana and Ambala, which have been mentioned as the two best positions, are, both of them, distant nearly twelve hundred miles from Calcutta, and almost as many from Bombay; but as measures are now in progress to open the navigation of the Indus and its tributaries, and as Lodiana stands on the navigable waters of the Sutledge, one of its principal branches, and as there is now a plan on foot for a steam communication from Bombay to England, through the Mediterranean and the Red Sea, this part of India, and especially Lodiana, may eventually become of more easy and frequent access to us than Calcutta itself.

"Of the climate, and government, and inhabitants of the province of Lahore, it is stated that it consists of two parts: the one of which is the mountainous tract in the northeast, stretching south and east from Cashmere; and the other comprising the low and flat regions bounded on the south by the Sutledge, called the Punjab. The former has a climate much resembling that of middle Europe, but is thinly peopled in comparison to the other, which is by far the most productive, though less salubrious. It comprises a territory of seventy thousand square miles, and a population of several millions, and is said to contain many fine villages and some large towns; but those of the latter, with the exception of Amritsar, the holy city of the Sikhs, are in a declining condition. Lahore is under the government of a native ruler by the name of Runjeet Singh, formerly one of the most formidable enemies of the Anglo-Indian government, but now on terms of friendship with it.

"The political changes which have recently taken place in respect to India, the increasing desire of persons of distinction among the natives to give their children an English education, and the disposition of the constituted authorities to encourage the settlement of educated and intelligent missionaries in all parts of that country, are to be regarded as truly auspicious circumstances.

"The brethren readily obtained permission of the Governor-General of India to reside in the province which they had selected; but as the season least favorable for making the journey was about to commence, and as they could spend the intervening time profitably in the study of the language, they had concluded, on consultation with their friends in Calcutta, to remain in the vicinity of that city until June next."

IN CALCUTTA. [It was not the purpose of the missionaries to make any long stay in Calcutta; but the deeply sorrowful illness and bereavement, referred to on preceding pages, caused considerable detention. Afterwards it was fully learned that the best time for beginning the 1,000 miles of the voyage on the Ganges was at the commencement of the rainy season, several months later. This unexpected delay involved little if any disadvantage in learning the Hindustani language; many people from the up-country provinces were living in that city. But other things of importance had to be studied by new missionaries of a Society itself new. Climatic conditions affecting health; methods of business; social usages of natives and foreigners; the religious systems of the Hindus as exemplified in daily life—all required practical attention. The work of missions, moreover, in its varied methods, as conducted by several Christian denominations and about twenty missionaries, called for careful and thoughtful study. It is well therefore to introduce a few notices of missionary topics suggested by this temporary abode in the capital city. And in connection therewith reference may be made to a book published in 1850—"Two Years in Upper India." It gives information, partly personal, largely general, concerning what was expected to be the life work of the writer, but what proved to be chiefly the pioneer work of the mission. The Notes of the present book may be viewed as suggested by or connected with the interests of the Lodiana Mission.

MISSIONARIES AND OTHER FRIENDS. Among the missionaries and other gentlemen, then in Calcutta, or its immediate vicinity, were men of eminent ability and scholarship, whose counsels were of great service to the new missionaries. Some of them had lived many years in India, and all of them were held in esteem for their Christian character. Such men as Drs. Carey and Marshman; Archdeacon Corrie, afterwards Bishop of Madras, Henry Martyn's friend, not in missionary ranks, but of a devoted missionary spirit; Drs. Yates and Duff; Messrs. Pearce, Lacroix, Mackey, Ewart, Ellis, Mather, and others; besides the Scotch chaplain, Dr. Charles, and the Evangelical Bishop, Dr. Wilson; Col. Dunlop, an elder in the Scotch church; and Mr. afterwards Sir Charles Trevelyan, one of the secretaries of the Government. The revered Archdeacon, Col. Dunlop, and Mr. Trevelyan had been stationed for several years in the northwestern provinces, and they were well acquainted with that part of the country and its people. The information received from them, most kindly given, was invaluable. At the suggestion of the secretary, one of the missionaries and himself spent a day at Barrackpore, and were invited to dine at the palace. The Governor-General was on a visit to a distant part of the country, but Lady Bentinck was very kind in her reception of her guests, and made a most pleasing impression of herself and of her interest in the Christian welfare of the people of India. Her example and that of Lord Cavendish Bentinck promoted all that was good for the Hindus. Their friendly influence greatly favored our missionary work in the northwest provinces.

CORDIAL INTERCOURSE OF MISSIONARIES. Nothing could exceed the cordial intercourse of the missionaries of different churches with each other, as shown on all occasions; this was very evident at their monthly meeting. It was held for breakfast at each other's homes, their wives always with them when they could come. After this social hour the ladies were left to the pleasant service of entertaining each other, while the men went to the study, for conference on subjects of common interest. It might be to consider a special paper, read by previous appointment; or a matter requiring consideration in the occurrences of the previous month; or the composing informally of some local trouble between native Christians of different missions; or settling plans for common missionary services, etc. A marked example of this good feeling occurred. The best translation of the New Testament in Bengali had been recently completed by the eminent Sanscrit and Bengali scholar, the Rev. Dr. Yates, of the English Baptist Mission. His Baptist co-laborers were grateful for it and proud of it, as well they might be. It was printed at their press in Calcutta, and its merits became known to the missionaries of other denominations, so that a strong desire existed to be permitted to make use of it in their work. But certain words stood in the way; many could not use *immerse* as the only Scriptural word in English or Bengali for baptism. The case received friendly consultation, and in good time permission was cordially given to print this superior version separately, with certain words *transferred* as in our English version, while the Baptist brethren continued to print them according to their usage. All honor to them for their Christian spirit! The suggestion may be added, that words denoting ideas or objects not in a native language might in several cases be transferred, and not translated according to a common Hindu usage. As an example, " tea kettle " was not in use. The people did not drink tea, the word kettle was not known, until foreigners came to live in India; and the word itself has two sounds not expressed in their alphabet—the open and the obtuse sounds of *e*. The people solved the difficulty by *transferring* the word, writing it "kitlee," and so naturalizing it as a Hindu word, with an easy and accurate idea of its meaning. Might not some of our Christian words, such as "righteousness, sanctification, and redemption," be transferred in like manner?

The harmony of the Calcutta Conference should rebuke an error as to personal "difficulties" among missionaries. The writer of these lines may say that he heard of no difficulties as resulting from their being of so many denominations. After many years of observation he believes that difficulties hardly ever do occur among missionaries; and when unhappily they occur, it is usually among men of *their own missions*. In too close relations to each other, men of imperfectly sanctified nature may give or take umbrage where no offence was intended, or ought not to have been given. More grace would prevent or terminate the trouble. Let all be "meek and lowly in heart," as Christ was, and there will never be any personal difficulties. But if difficulties do arise, then let Matthew xviii. 15-17, and Luke vi. 31, be deeply considered, and literally followed.

TRUE IDEA OF CHRISTIAN UNION. Before passing from this Conference it may be referred to as manifesting the true idea and the duty of Christian union. Our Saviour's prayer, John xvii. 11 and 21, was heard for these missionaries. Of the five denominations in Calcutta, each missionary followed the line of life and of work for Christ to which he felt himself called, or to which his Home Church had appointed him. No one attempted to break down denominational lines of Church order and worship. These could be maintained in charity and in deference to the differing views of other brethren. This separate action as members of different missionary societies was not antagonistic, nor intentionally divisive; neither was it weakening. It was like the infantry, cavalry, artillery, etc., of an army—increasing, not lessening, its power; it was one in purpose, object, and sympathy. It was all this because it was a spiritual union —like that of the sacred Persons in the Blessed Trinity. In the work of redemption, their offices are separate, and yet they are one. Many are the orders of the angels, moreover, and many the high services of the archangels, differing, but all one in spirit, aim, and end. The kingdom of God cometh not with observation—not with outward show and parade; it is "within you." More perfect spiritual union will yet be obtained. In the meantime missionaries are to be chiefly "witnesses unto Christ," standing firmly in the truth, as they have received it, and regarding those from whom they differ in this respect as "the weaker brethren"; while yet willing to be so regarded by them. But as they learn more of divine truth, they will stand more nearly to the same standards.

CHIEF WORK OF MISSIONARIES. The members of the Conference stood in the lines of the apostles—as their chief work was the preaching of the Gospel. If educational labors were adopted, it was still for direct, evangelizing purposes. If tracts, or books, or translations of the Scriptures were prepared, it was not for literary or scholastic reputation; nothing but Christ and Him crucified was kept in view. In all respects, in the use of all their gifts, they might have said with Spurgeon: "I hate the science of comparative theology. I know but one God, and all the rest are idols. I hate the comparison of sacred books. I know of only one, and all the rest are pretenders." A greater than Spurgeon once stood on Mars Hill, far superior to all his hearers, in gifts of intellect, learning, and oratory; and he declared to them the true God; he spent little time on their "comparative" theories and criticisms. He would know nothing but Christ and Him crucified. Even so let every missionary and every friend of missions abide in the singleness of Gospel service! In accord with this good wish was the teaching of the late Dr. Charles Hodge on Atheism, Pantheism, Polytheism, etc. (Systematic Theology, vol. i.); and the works of Sir Monier Williams on Brahmanism, Hinduism, and Buddhism as an outgrowth of the latter,—two vols., by the foremost scholar of our day on such subjects, and a reverent disciple of our Saviour. Such studies by such men may be of great use to a few persons of special gifts; but hardly if in Sanscrit, to most missionaries.

HINDU SCHOLARS.
THE POOR.
THE OUTLOOK.
The native Hindu scholars of eminence seldom learn to rest in Christ Jesus for salvation. A more remarkable example could hardly be cited than that of Raja Rammohun Roy, whose death on a visit in England was reported in Calcutta in 1834, after a long life of eminent scholarship and fairness, especially in the line of Comparative Religions, as to which his writings were indeed remarkable. He ended his course virtually as a Unitarian, but he remained to the last a Brahman. Some of his disciples adhered to his teaching. Eventually their views were represented in the Brahma Somáj, or Society —not properly called a Church; and other Somájas were formed in various provinces, particularly the Arya Somáj. Their leading adherents have usually acquired some degree of education in English; many of them

have given up the grosser features of idolatry, and profess to find the true idea of religion in the early history of their sacred writings. But they all, or nearly all, remain in the bonds of caste, and seldom become followers of the Saviour of sinners. These Somáj Hindus are comparatively but a small part of the two hundred and ninety millions of the Hindus.

Nevertheless great changes have taken place in India within the last century. The people are now under the best government and the most upright rulers, and enjoy the best means of education, they have ever had. Foreign commerce, railroads, steamboats, all work against caste; and many modern ideas are penetrating minds long contented in darkness. Particular statements cannot here be adduced; but as yet it must be acknowledged that the masses of the Hindus, the poorer classes forming the great bulk of the inhabitants, know but little of the Gospel. It is, however, among the poorer Hindus that the chief encouragement has been found in missionary work—among the poorer castes, the Teloogoos, for instance, or the almost no-castes like the Chuhras. Our missionary life and work in India, as in every country, is of course for all—high and low, rich and poor, Brahmans and Chuhras, as it was in the days of Schwartz, Carey, Spurgeon, and the great Apostle. Such indeed was the example of our blessed Lord himself. In His teaching we see little if any reference to the speculations of Roman, Grecian, and other so-called philosophers, but the principles and truths that He taught overthrew all their vain theories; He preached the Gospel to the poor. Such preaching will carry the victory over every form of error, from the Vale of Cashmere to Cape Comorin, and to the ends of the earth.

EXCEPTIONABLE THEORIES. In this period an Independent missionary, who had been ten or a dozen of years in another country, passed through Calcutta on his way to his home in Europe. He held the opinions of the Darbyites, or Plymouth Brethren, made but little of church organization and its ministry, expected the speedy coming of our Saviour, and believed that the world would *then* soon be converted. He was a man of talents, pleasing manners, and a fine conversationalist. A kind and courteous reception was accorded to him by individuals; but his confident opinions, strongly expressed to men who were his seniors in experience and of greater practical ability as missionaries, limited the influence of his visit. It was an example to be studied by a new missionary, particularly its questionable trust in unusual methods, and its expectation of immediate success. His hopes have not been verified. A somewhat similar theory as to haste in the salvation of the world is now advocated in certain quarters. This, it is held, can be done "before the end of this century," or at any rate, "during this generation." It is to be done by *evangelizing*, not by *converting*, the world. Now whatever limited instruction might be given in times of persecution by the disciples of Christ fleeing for their lives, we must refer to our Lord's last commandment as the foundation of Christian missions. Such is the faith of the Church in all ages. This commandment is obeyed by Teaching and by the administration of Baptism. "Go ye therefore and make disciples of all the nations," Baptizing them, and Teaching them. (See Revised version, and margin of Authorized version.) These requirements are understood to include church organization, the ministry, the succession of Gospel ordinances, and the use of the means of grace.

So the Commandment was understood by the Apostles; so by the first Christians (see Acts xiii.). And such is the general understanding of our Presbyterian people at the present day. It is "power from on high" that will qualify men to be missionaries and give them success; it is as "witnesses unto Christ" they go forth, in the use of the appointed means of grace; it is far from being merely flying heralds, "not stopping even to repeat the rejected message." As to the exact time of the world's redemption, we may well leave that with God. Has it been revealed unto us? Let the wonderful progress of missionary work in our day call forth grateful acknowledgment, and be continued with true devotion, on only Scriptural lines and promises!

PAINFUL SIGHTS. The sojourn of the new missionaries at the chief city of India, gave them numberless opportunities of seeing the influence of heathenism on its inhabitants. It is dark and dreadful; yet the people are an interesting race, and their land one of the best in the world. But illustrations cannot here be given, though an incident or two may be mentioned. One of the painful "sights" at Howrah, opposite Calcutta, where the missionaries lived for several months, was that of "hook-swinging,"—not then prohibited by the Government. This case occurred on a vacant lot in the rear of their house—not many feet distant, but in full view from their back windows. The poor man was evidently intoxicated, and hardly conscious of what was going on. A thick bandage around his waist, covering the space in which the hooks were inserted in his back, prevented the risk of being thrown to the ground. The hooks were pushed into the living flesh, and tied by strong cords to the end of a slender cross-beam of twenty-five or thirty feet. This beam was fastened and made to revolve on the top of an upright post about thirty feet high. It was then rapidly pulled around and around by spectators seizing the ropes fastened to its other end—swinging the poor victim in the air, flourishing a cane in bravado for several minutes. The shouts of the crowd saluted him. When he was let down, he appeared to be stupid and unconscious, but he was looked on as a martyr. It was a painful, irreverent, disgusting sight, worthy of heathenism.

Of many sad sights, none was more touching than that of a young mother teaching her little daughter to worship an idol. On his early morning walk for exercise in the suburbs, when but few persons were yet in the street, one of the missionaries saw this young woman going with a serious air and holding in hand a child four or five years old, which was trying hard to keep up. Leaving the street, she entered a small, open space, and stood at the door of a low temple. There she made her own worship, bowing down, then she took her child's hands, put them together, and raised them to its face, and taught the little girl to salute the idol. A few minutes were thus spent, and, after leaving some small gift for the idol, or rather, for the attending priest, they slowly left the place, and returned to the street homeward. The missionary went into the enclosed place, looked into the house of the idol, but could hardly recognize its hideous features in the dim light. From this his thoughts followed the poor mother and her little daughter, and deeply was his morning walk saddened. How little were her anxious thoughts for her dear child relieved! How dark was her mind! Alas for the heathen mother and the heathen child!]

In the Second Annual Report, 1834, already quoted, the missionaries are referred to as "expressing, and that repeatedly, the hope that additional missionaries may be speedily sent out to join them; and the decease of one of their valued members, and the importance of the field itself, give great force to this solicitation. The Committee are happy to say that they have it in prospect to send a reinforcement in the course of the ensuing autumn. In the meantime, it would be highly useful to provide for that station a printing-press to be sent out from this country, with the view of obtaining a font of type in the Punjabee at Calcutta; and charts, maps, and globes, and other apparatus, for the High School which the mission intend speedily to establish, would be extremely serviceable. 'If one hundred additional missionaries could be sent out there would be,' say these brethren, 'an abundance of work to employ them all.'"

The following quotations are from the Third Annual Report, of May 18, 1835:

"Our last Report left its three surviving members, viz., the Rev. John C. Lowrie, Rev. William Reed, and Mrs. Harriet Reed, in Calcutta, diligently prosecuting the study of the language of the Punjab; and making preparations to leave that city for the North of India, as soon as the appropriate season should arrive. In the meantime, however, the health of Mr. Reed became visibly impaired, and a bad cough and fever were soon followed by the painful evidences of a confirmed consumption. From this period, the decline of this amiable and devoted missionary was so rapid, that all expectation of his being able to labor in India ceased; and after long and trying consultation, and after having obtained the best medical advice, it was resolved that Mr. Reed and his partner should take passage for the United States, while Mr. Lowrie proceeded to Lodiana, to make preparations to commence the mission.

"Mr. and Mrs. Reed embarked on the 23d of July (1834), and on the 12th of August, after a few days of rapid decline, the dying missionary closed in serenity and peace his earthly sufferings, and his remains in the evening of the same day were committed to the watery deep; leaving his bereaved partner in the most delicate and trying circumstances, to prosecute the tedious voyage on which they had just entered. The gratitude of the Board is due to Captain Land of the ship *Edward*, for his affectionate sympathy and unremitting attention to Mr. Reed while he survived, and to his widowed companion, who reached this country in safety on the 12th of December following.

"Mr. Lowrie left Calcutta on the day after this painful separation from his beloved associates, and, at the date of his last communications, had arrived within a few days' travel of Lodiana [arriving there November 5, 1834], having ascended the Ganges to Cawnpore, and thus gained by personal observation much useful information, as to the state of society and morals, the customs and religious rites of the Hindus, the trade and various phenomena of that far-famed river, and of the scenery, soil, productions, cities, temples, and military stations, along its banks.

"In view of the providential reduction of this mission to a single individual, it is cause of unfeigned thankfulness to God that the survivor, and the pioneer in the enterprise, should be a man who, by the union of judgment, prudence, and energy, with gentleness, fortitude, and devotedness to the work, is so well fitted for the difficult and responsible situation.

"In the beginning of November last, the Rev.

Messrs. James Wilson and John Newton, with their wives, and Miss Julia A. Davis, sailed from Boston as a reinforcement to this mission; and probably ere this have arrived at Calcutta, from whence, after becoming acquainted with the friends of missions in that city, and making the necessary preparations, they are expected to proceed in time to join Mr. Lowrie early in autumn. The Rev. James R. Campbell, of the Reformed Presbyterian Church, and the Rev. James McEwen, of the Presbytery of Philadelphia, and Mr. David Hull, licentiate of the Presbytery of Northumberland, have since been appointed to the same field, and are expected, in connection with a physician, and one or two assistant teachers, if suitable persons should in the meantime be obtained, to leave this country in October next. If this reinforcement be permitted to reach Lodiana in safety, and not find the force already sent out materially weakened, it is the expectation of the Committee that an additional station, either in Cashmere, at Ambala, or some still more promising position, will be soon formed. Through the distinguished munificence of a single individual, an excellent philosophical apparatus for a native high-school has already been sent to Upper India, and it is the purpose of the Committee to provide a printing-press and apparatus, to be forwarded next fall; and from the number of young men who are known to have that field in view, and other indications of Providence in reference to it, they are led to believe that these and every other desirable facility for the vigorous and extended prosecution of this mission, should be provided. In view of the disproportionate amount of effort which the Committee have already resolved to apply to Northwestern India, the Board may desire a brief statement of the considerations on which this policy is founded [as drawn from books on India and Central Asia, not from the correspondence of the missionaries, then too recently arrived to write on some of these subjects]. They are such as apply to Hindustan in general, and such as respect that part of it in particular.

"It is in the contemplation of India, and with it as an instrument, the whole of peninsular Asia, as apparently on the eve of a great revolution in its intellectual and religious prospects, that we feel a special interest in it as a missionary field. If the train of causes which led to the establishment and the extension of a Protestant power in that country, and which will inevitably lead to the far greater extension of its moral influence, and develop the singular wisdom of Divine Providence, not less so are now the means by which the fearful structure of Buddhism is crumbling away. The native press, originally got up to sustain it, is now, through its concessions and the tone of feeling it encourages, becoming a most powerful engine in its overthrow. It now contributes with other means, to weaken prejudices and soften the asperities of bigotry; to excite a spirit of inquiry; and is, with the influence of native schools, creating a thirst for knowledge, and making Christianity a topic of familiar conversation, tending to aid the civil authority in the suppression of those cruelties and excesses, by which superstition maintains its firmest hold of an ignorant and deluded people. The Brahmans, it is said, fully expect the speedy termination of all the sanctity of their idolized rivers; and then, as one of them recently observed, 'nothing will remain to Hindus but to embrace the Christian faith.' If this is the feeling beginning to possess the minds of the most bigoted and influential among a population of one hundred and twenty millions, and that in a land which has been the stronghold of Buddhism, and at a moment when Burmah, on its border, is also powerfully shaken, we may easily see how eventful to the missionary enterprise is the crisis which it has attained.

"We, however, proceed to notice the local advantages of Northern India.

"In the execution of the Redeemer's commission, no part of the earth, it is true, is to be excepted, on account of the insalubrity of its climate or the degradation or the ferocity of its population. Still, at every stage of the progress of its evangelization, it is proper, other things being equal, to prefer locations of less moral or physical obstruction, to those which have greater. The intense heat and periodical winds of the day, and the extreme humidity of the atmosphere, in the wet seasons of Hindustan, have always made almost every part of it a precarious and very often a fatal abode, for both Anglo and American emigrants; although the cold is doubtless considerably greater in these upper provinces, than in other parts of India. Burns found the heat so great at Lahore, Lodiana, and Moultan, that in the month of June the thermometer stood at 100°, even in the shade of a bungalow artificially cooled. The chief consideration, therefore, in favor of this field, is its proximity to some of the most elevated and salubrious posts in Asia. Simla, a place of considerable resort for sanitary purposes, which attains an elevation of 7,800 feet above the level of the sea, and where, according to Captain Mundy, the thermometer in May or June never rises higher than 72°, and never sinks lower than 55°, is but 100 miles from Lodiana. Roopur and Sabathu are still nearer, while Ambala, which has been sometimes mentioned by our brethren for a second position, approaches still closer to the base of the Asiatic range. If, in securing these advantages of locality, we have receded several hundreds of miles into the interior, ordinarily precluding frequent communication, and requiring a long and expensive journey, it is to be recollected that 1,000 miles in the navigation of rivers destitute of every obstruction, will bring the trade of the Punjab, as high up as Lodiana, to the ocean, on the line of the intended thoroughfare from India to Europe—not less than 1,000 miles nearer the latter than Calcutta itself. [A hope since verified, though not by navigation, but by railway. The journey to either city is now made in two or three days.]

"Apart from the fact that the opening of the Indus and its tributaries to an active commerce by steam communication, now in contemplation, and the concentration of a considerable trade from Thibet and Tartary, through the defiles of the mountains, carrying back into these benighted regions the arts and religious light of Christian nations, it is to be observed, that the political ascendency of the powerful chief of the Sikh nation, already makes the Punjab the most safe and convenient entrance into Cabool, Bokhara, and Eastern Persia. In these countries, it is true, the Moslem faith, in a milder form than in Western Asia, has long prevailed; but it is believed that Christianity would even now be tolerated, as Hinduism is; and Burns states that while travelling in these unfrequented countries, he gathered from the conversation of the Mohammedans of Cabool and Persia among themselves, that there existed among them a prediction that Christianity was speedily to overturn the entire structure of their faith. The Scriptures have been translated into the Mongolian language—a language spoken by many tribes, from the shores of the Baikal to the borders of Thibet, and from the Caspian to the gates of Pekin, including millions in the Chinese empire; and if our Society should eventually establish a mission at Selinga, Kiatka, or some other spot under the protection of a Christian power, in Asiatic Russia, and another on the borders of China or Tartary, on the great thoroughfare from Pekin to Tobolsk and St. Petersburgh, these two remote positions would stand towards each other, and the great plateau of Central Asia, in the most interesting and powerful relation."

[In the earlier years of the India Mission the journey of a family, and of a single traveller with any housekeeping articles, from Calcutta to Lodiana, was made by boat on the Ganges to Cawnpore or to Futtehgurh—the former about 620 miles direct distance or 1,000 miles by the river, requiring about two months and a half for the voyage; the latter 720 miles direct; and then overland to Lodiana, nearly 1,200 miles from Calcutta. For the tedious, dangerous, but very interesting river journey; and for information concerning Upper India and the first years of the new mission, see the book already referred to.

AT LODIANA, MESSRS. WILSON AND NEWTON. From the 23d of November, 1835, to the 21st of January, 1836, the first three missionaries, above named, had the happiness of meeting again and spending the time mostly at Lodiana. They and Mr. Reed had been personal friends at college and theological seminary. They had been separated in the spring of 1833. Sad changes had since occurred. But now with the lovely and devoted Mrs. Wilson and Mrs. Newton they were in Christian fellowship and council, in regard to the cause of Christ, in the great field set before the Church which they represented.

Mr. Wilson was a man of sterling good sense, bright, and genial, of most winning manners, and of truly consecrated spirit; Mr. Newton was of humble, straightforward devotedness to the cause of Christ, and of considerate and most pleasant address. And it is paying the ladies an insufficient compliment to say that they were worthy of their husbands. All are entered into rest except the writer of these lines.

Of their ten children, six entered the ministry, of whom two were also physicians; one was an elder, two were wives of missionaries, and one was the wife of a merchant, both faithful members of the Church—seven of them in foreign or home missionary service, one an honored pastor at home for many years in his present charge—all showing a good and enviable record; so one may write who has kept a friendly eye on them all. Of these ten, five have gone to be in the blessed family of heaven.

WHY A PRESBYTERY WAS NOT FORMED AT LODIANA. Many subjects were carefully studied in this council of five persons, with earnest prayers for divine direction. For information as to most of these matters reference may be made to the Annual Reports of the Society and to the pages of its monthly magazine—the *Foreign Missionary Chronicle*. One of these subjects, however, does not appear to have been reported, and it is worthy of a place in this Note. Why did not the three ministers organize a Presbytery at Lodiana? It was not for want of a high regard for this part of their Church system, nor for any inferior sense of its bearing on their work as missionaries; but it was mainly owing to their inexperience,—and perhaps to some want of consideration at home. At any rate the young ministers supposed that organized churches and ruling elders were required as well as ministers, in order to constitute a Presbytery. This view was not accepted in this country, as they afterwards learned. See the two Presbyteries organized in California, one by each General Assembly, old and new, each Presbytery at first consisting only of ministers. On the theory that the office of a minister includes that of an elder, this action was "in order"; as it might have been at any rate in the special circumstances. And it is a matter of regret that this ruling could not have been known at Lodiana; a Presbytery would then have been organized in 1835, instead of 1842; with the approval of the General Assembly.

This revered institution might have modified what is known as the *Mission*, afterwards so prominent; or it might perhaps have altogether prevented its coming into use among Presbyterians, abroad as at home.

PRESBYTERY ON MISSION. In the next company of missionaries for the Lodiana field, several Reformed Presbyterian missionaries, and others of the same Church afterwards, led to their organizing a Presbytery in connection with their Synod, while the earlier brethren and their successors eventually formed a Presbytery connected with the General Assembly. Subsequently most of the Reformed Presbyterian brethren, and ministers and elders of their Synod, among the best men, found their ecclesiastical home in the Presbyterian Church. In all this, there was no want of agreement and Christian fellowship. It led partly, however, to the transaction of certain missionary matters by the 'Mission,' rather than by the Presbytery, following in this respect the example of other Societies, earlier in the field, who were supported mostly by Congregational or Independent churches.

The question has often been asked, whether the

so-called 'Missions' of the Presbyterian Church might not well be superseded by Presbyteries. It is a subject that has several sides, and it is not intended to discuss it here at any length. So far as financial matters are concerned, the native ministers and elders might well have the Presbyterial supervision of gifts and payments of funds from the native churches and other native sources, their votes by common consent being necessary to a decision. In like manner the foreign members should continue in charge of the funds sent out by the churches in our country, as best understanding their conditions, readily being held responsible for their specified use, and best aiding to obtain liberal support for the work. It is moreover of great interest, that the common consideration and discussion by both the native and foreign brethren in Presbytery would go far to prepare the native churches for their great work of self-support, when they become independent of foreign assistance. The 'Mission' is but a Committee of a Committee, consisting of foreign members. The Presbytery is of divine warrant, abroad as at home. It includes all, native and foreign, ministers and elders. It acts under definite rules —well known, easily applicable to all cases, and subject to review. The present double action of Mission and Presbytery seems to require a good deal of *adjusting*. It certainly seems to be important that ministers and elders of native churches should be on the same general footing with their foreign brethren, in matters affecting the welfare of their churches. And it is gratifying to feel sure that this is the common feeling on both sides.

There is a home side to the question of Presbytery instead of Mission. The latter seems to require greater labors at the Mission House and greater expense also than would be incurred by the former. This results from placing the supervision of so many matters in the charge of the Executive officers. Important duties must certainly devolve upon the Board as a Permanent Committee of the General Assembly, such as the apportionment of funds among the fields of labor, the appointment of missionaries, etc. But the methods of work *in the field*, the numberless details of this work already to some extent under their supervision, might well be left as far as possible to the missionaries; as also the general subjects that fall under the settled policy of the Church in this country. These brethren are capable of such work, being the equals of their fellow-laborers at home. These field matters must have due attention—which could be best secured, as it is believed, under the Presbytery, rather than the Mission. And all the more so, as the number of missionaries becomes larger, their experience increased, and their plans of work fully matured. On the other hand, the more limited supervision at home would be increasingly thorough, and involve less expense.

Purposely this suggestion leaves out of view expenses for the collection of funds in this country. On the theory of our Church, elsewhere referred to, gifts for the cause of Missions are the fruits of divine grace, and should be sought for mainly in the use of the ordinary means of grace, under the lead of the church session and pastor. Many and remarkable examples verifying this might be readily cited in our Presbyterian churches. The good influence of all our church courts, Presbyteries, Synods, and the General Assembly, greatly promotes this happy result. Where this general Church influence is adverse, a Missionary Society is justifiable in the employment of agencies in visits to churches that may be open to them for collections; as in the case of a foreign Society, which is admirably conducted, though its agents are much larger in number than its Executive officers, and their expense greater.

The line of policy as to supervision thus briefly suggested was the well-considered opinion of the late senior Secretary of the oldest Missionary Board in our country, a minister eminent for his great knowledge and discriminating judgment in missionary affairs. It was based on intimate and long acquaintance with Missions in his own Church. He believed that in this way the number of missionaries might be largely increased without a proportional increase of executive expenses in this country. In the Presbyterian denomination we may prefer Presbytery to Missions, for many reasons; but in both let the supervision of the work in the field be left to the men on the ground as far as practicable.]

The following extracts are from the Fourth Annual Report, May, 1836, from the pen of Dr. Swift:

"This mission at present, consists of fifteen individuals, comprising five ordained ministers of the Gospel and three candidates for the ministry, and possessing two printing-presses, a philosophical apparatus, and a good library. The Committee rejoice in being able to state, that since the last Annual Report, the operations of the Mission to India have been attended with the continued marks of the divine favor. The lives of all the missionaries have been preserved, and the health of the Rev. John C. Lowrie, the only one of them who has been seriously indisposed, has not materially changed during the year. Rev. Messrs. James Wilson and John Newton, with their wives, after a prosperous voyage, arrived at Calcutta in due season, and remained in that city, as was expected, until the 24th of June last, when they proceeded by water, on their way to the Upper Provinces. During their stay, and on their protracted voyage up the

Ganges, they were all blessed with good health and spirits; at the last date of intelligence from them, they were proceeding, by land, from the river to Lodiana, where they probably arrived early in December last. Miss Julia A. Davis, who accompanied this reinforcement, as an assistant to the mission, was induced, some time after her arrival at Calcutta, and with the concurrence of our brethren, and the friends of the missionary cause in that city, to form a matrimonial connection with Rev. John Goadby, of the English General Baptist Mission at Cuttack; and in consequence withdrew from her connection with this Board, with the hope, it is believed, of being enabled, with greater prospects of usefulness, to prosecute the work for which she left her native land.

"Our missionary brethren appear to have met with great kindness and hospitality, at all the stations and British settlements, on their way up the Ganges, and to have experienced a growing conviction of the importance of India missions, and the desirableness of a great enlargement of our operations in that country.

"Mr. Lowrie having, in compliance with a special and repeated invitation from the powerful sovereign of the Punjab, made an excursion to the court of Lahor, conferred with the Government on the subject of education, and visited some of the principal cities and other objects of interest within its territory; and having spent the hot season at Simla, in what is familiarly called the Hills, or Hill Provinces, and made several tours of observation during the summer, for the purposes of information as well as of exercise and change of air, has thus collected an amount of knowledge which may prove highly useful to the cause of missions.

"In education, agriculture, and morals, Mr. Lowrie found the population of the Maha Rajah, Runjeet

Singh, consisting of Sikhs, Hindus, Mussulmans, etc., much like other parts of Hindustan. This territory was originally divided among a number of independent princes, who now acknowledge the sway of this powerful chief. But on the termination of his life, now considerably advanced, it is supposed that things will revert to their original condition; and the whole eventually fall, as other portions of India have done, under the direction of the British power.

"A considerable part of the country through which Mr. Lowrie passed, is neither fertile nor densely populated; but the vicinity of the capital was covered with luxuriant wheat and fine gardens, extremely fertile, and adorned with the beautiful mango and tamarind trees. Amritsir, the seat of Sikh learning and devotion, the resort of pilgrims, and the site of a beautiful and picturesque sacred reservoir, is important also, as the commercial emporium of the Punjab, and the mart of the fine fabrics of Cashmere; and may thus be regarded as the most eligible position in Lahor for a missionary station, whenever our operations in that quarter shall demand a selection. The result of Mr. Lowrie's observations, however, would seem, for the present, to give a decided preference to the population of the Hill provinces, as, in some respects, more likely to be benefited by missionary efforts, and as possessing a climate more favorable to the health of missionaries. The people are less attached to caste than those of the Plains, and to those immoral habits and customs which so extensively abound in India; being simple in their habits and modes of life, devoted to agriculture, and combining a larger share of industry, uprightness, and thoughtfulness of character. The natural productions of the soil, and consequently the staple articles of subsistence, correspond also much more with those of our own country; and this fact, while it might promote both the comfort and the health of our missionaries, would enable them to transfer to this simple-hearted people, and introduce among them, many of the improvements in agriculture and horticulture which exist in their native land."

The Third Annual Report, 1835, continues:

"In November last, a second reinforcement, consisting of Rev. James McEwen, of the Associate Reformed Synod; Rev. James R. Campbell, of the Synod of the Reformed Presbyterian Church, with their wives; and Messrs. William Rogers and Joseph Porter, graduates of Miami University; and Mr. Jesse S. Jamieson, graduate of Jefferson College, with their wives, sailed from Philadelphia, in the ship *Charles Wharton*, for Calcutta; and, at the date of the last advices, these ten brethren and sisters, with Rev. Messrs. Winslow and Dwight, and their wives, of the American Board, were all in good health, and expected to reach their destined port about the first of March last. Neither of the three last named brethren of this reinforcement had prosecuted a regular course of theological education, before leaving this country; though each had completed his academical course with uncommon respectability, as to scholarship and correct moral and religious deportment. From information previously received, and of high authority, the Committee were led to believe that these brethren, by spending a few of the first years of their missionary labors as teachers, in the higher departments of education in India, might promote the great object of its evangelization, as effectually as any other; and that, while an entrance upon these pursuits, fresh from the studies of an academic education, and with a view to enter the holy ministry as soon as they should be prepared for it, and the progress of the mission might demand it, would bring them more speedily into active service, it would not materially affect their prospective usefulness as ambassadors of Christ to the heathen.

"Two printing-presses and fonts of type, as well in the Roman character as that of the principal languages of the Northern Provinces of Hindustan, have in the meantime been sent forward; and Mr. Reese Morris, of Philadelphia, a practical printer, with his wife, has been accepted as an assistant in the mission, and is expected to repair to India with the next reinforcement. In the intervening time, provision has been made to employ the service of printers on the spot, and a very considerable portion of the expense of this part of our establishment in India will be defrayed, by the publication of a paper about to be established by the British agent at Lodiana. On the arrival of this reinforcement at the station, it is expected that the missionaries, after all due inquiry and observation has been made, will so divide and arrange their forces as to occupy one or two additional positions.

"The Rev. Mr. Lowrie, having suffered considerably from impaired health during most of the time of his residence in India, and having been advised by his physicians to return and spend a year or two in this country, received some months ago from the Committee permission to do so, and, if no material change should have since occurred, his return to the United States may be anticipated during the course of the present year."

[The Fifth Annual Report of the Western Foreign Missionary Society, May 1, 1837, was prepared by the Hon. Walter Lowrie. He succeeded Dr. Swift as Corresponding Secretary of this Society. Born in Edinburgh in 1784, he was in his father's large family when they emigrated to this country in 1792. He was brought up on a farm, and assisted his father in a saw-mill, to which a flour-mill was afterwards added, in Butler County, Pennsylvania. Becoming an earnest member of the church, he engaged in studies for the ministry, and made good progress in learning the Latin, Greek, and Hebrew languages; but it became evident that his studies should be laid aside, and he then engaged in teaching a school in the county town. This led to his becoming known, and then to his being elected to the Senate of Pennsylvania repeatedly for seven years; he was then elected to the Senate of the United States, 1818-1824; and afterwards as Secretary of the United States Senate, 1824-1836.

Under the usage of that time he might have continued to occupy this office; but he resigned it to become Secretary of the Missionary Society. He had at first declined this appointment, but felt constrained to accept it, a year later, on its being renewed. In this new sphere of duty he had the full sympathy and preference of his beloved wife. He had always maintained his religious character and convictions. It was in this consecrated life that consent was given to his eldest son, and afterwards to two younger sons, going as missionaries. In the case of the first he felt some hesitation, partly in view of the need of more ministers in our own country, and partly for reasons of health; but after careful thought his judgment became satisfied, and he encouraged him to enter on this work for Christ, as also in the case of his younger sons, notwithstanding the deep personal trial of these separations. His final acceptance of the missionary office was but in the same line of Christian duty. He continued in the Missionary

Secretaryship until his death in 1868—in the 85th year of his age.

His early training in practical work; his year of theological studies; his twenty-five years in public service; his membership on the Senate's Committee on Indian Affairs; his sons' questions of duty as to missionary life; his relations to the Church of Christ as a member and an elder, all it is now plain were tributary to his great work for life.]

Interesting notices concerning India are taken from this Report:

"This most extensive of the missions of the Society has continued to enjoy the protection and blessing of God. The only adverse circumstance is the return, on account of ill health, of the Rev. John C. Lowrie, as intimated in the last report. Mr. Lowrie left Lodiana the 20th January, 1836. When he arrived at Calcutta, it was found to be impracticable to obtain a passage direct to this country, and he was obliged to return by way of England. He arrived at New York the 28th December last. Since that time he has visited a number of the churches, making known the wants of the heathen, of whose perishing condition he has been an eye-witness. Should his health be restored, it is his settled purpose to return.

"The second reinforcement mentioned in the last report, consisting of Messrs. McEwen, Campbell, Rogers, Jamieson, Porter, and their wives, reached Calcutta in safety on the 1st of April. At Madras they parted with the Rev. Messrs. Winslow and Dwight, missionaries of the American Board, who were their companions in the voyage, and to whom they had become strongly attached in the bonds of Christian love and friendship. The joint labors of these brethren on the voyage were greatly blessed to the officers and sailors of the ship.

"On landing at Calcutta these brethren were greatly encouraged by meeting Mr. Lowrie. With his assistance they were soon accommodated with lodgings, and on the 27th June they commenced their voyage up the river. On the 1st November they had nearly reached their destination, with the exception of Mr. McEwen, who stopped at Allahabad with the intention of remaining there till spring.

"The Rev. Messrs. James Wilson and John Newton occupy the station at Lodiana. Besides the usual missionary labors, they have under their care the school first established at that station by the British Political Agent, Capt. Wade, but afterwards transferred to the care and direction of the mission. Capt. Wade is still its efficient patron, and the school at present gives high promise of service in the cause of the Redeemer. It consists of between forty and fifty youth, most of them from the first families. In this school everything which human means can provide is afforded for raising up an educated and qualified native ministry; and the Committee ask their fellow-Christians to join with them in daily prayer in pleading the promise of the Saviour (Luke xi. 9-13) for the gift of the Holy Spirit on the hearts of these youth. At this station are two printing-presses belonging to the Society.

"Besides Lodiana, two other stations—Sabathu and Saharunpur—have been selected, to be occupied by the last reinforcement.

"Sabathu, distant 110 miles northeast from Lodiana, is situated on the lower elevation of the Himalaya mountains, 4,000 feet above the level of the sea. Between the snowy ranges of these mountains and the plains of India there is an intervening tract of country, having an average breadth of about sixty miles, which, though mountainous in its character, is yet capable of cultivation to a considerable extent. A district in this hilly region, 200 miles in length, with a population of 250,000, is under the control of the East India Company. Sabathu is one of their military stations, and is considered an eligible point in regard to health, communication with other places, and general convenience for commencing the system of effort by which the Gospel is to be established over those mountain tribes.

"Saharunpur, distant 130 miles southeast from Lodiana, 100 miles north of Delhi, is situated within 20 miles of Hurdwar, that great rendezvous of pilgrims from all the surrounding nations. The annual fair at Hurdwar is attended by hundreds of thousands of all classes; and hitherto, with the exception of a few transient visits of a single missionary from Delhi, Satan has had the undisputed possession of this great field to himself. No place affords more advantages for the dissemination of the Sacred Scriptures and religious publications than the fair at Hurdwar. From this point they will be carried into the surrounding countries, and to all parts of Northern India, and even to the tribes beyond Cashmere, inhabiting the high table-lands of Central Asia.

"The Committee expected to have sent, early in the spring, to this important field, four additional missionaries. The Rev. Henry R. Wilson, Jr., and Mr. Reese Morris, Jr., a printer; and from the Reformed Presbyterian Church the Rev. Joseph Caldwell and Mr. James Craig, a teacher. But, owing to the want of funds, this reinforcement has been postponed till the coming fall. To it will then be added the Rev. John H. Morrison."

It may be proper to add here, that, agreeably to the intimation given above, these missionaries sailed for India in October, 1837.

"At Lodiana there are residing at present, under the protection of the British Government, two exiled kings from Afghanistan, who have their followers with them to the number of 2,000 or upward. There are also more than 3,500 Cashmerians residing at that station, and many at other towns in Upper India, who were driven from their native valley by famine and by the oppression of their rulers. They are employed in manufacturing the fine fabrics for which their country is so celebrated, and they retain the language and the usages of the tribe of the Hindu family to which they belong. Owing to the residence of these people at the principal missionary station, every opportunity is afforded of learning the language of those countries, and among them making known the way of forgiveness of sins through the risen Saviour. The opening of Divine Providence, in thus bringing such large portions of two nations who have never heard of Christ to the very door of missionary operations, was too plain to be neglected. One of the brethren of the next reinforcement will be appointed a missionary to Cashmere, and another of them to Afghanistan. Until they have learned the respective languages, these brethren will reside at Lodiana, and in every way endeavor to promote the best interests of those to whom they are sent.

"Mr. Morris will take charge of the printing-presses, and the two other brethren will occupy Ambala, Sirhind, or some of the other stations in the vicinity.

"The foregoing relation of facts and circumstances,

if there were no others, shows the importance of this region as a missionary field; but the half has not been told.

"It is a ground of no small encouragement, that here at least a Protestant mission has been planted, in advance of the missionaries of the Pope of Rome. Here too are the missionaries within a short distance of the hilly country, to which the sick and the invalid, without leaving missionary ground, may resort for health. On the west is the large and populous kingdom of the Punjab; with a population very similar to that among which the present stations are placed. On the borders of the Punjab are Cashmere and Afghanistan, those keys to the tribes inhabiting Central Asia. North and northeast from Lodiana, in the valleys stretching far into the recesses of the Himalaya mountains, are numerous tribes of Hindus, not more remarkable for their industry than for their quiet demeanor, the simplicity of their habits, and the almost imperceptible change which time has made upon their national customs. Stretching far to the southeast, between the snowy mountains and the plains, embracing the secondary range of the Himalaya mountains, is the kingdom of Nepaul. On the south is Rajpootana; and on the southwest, on both sides of the Indus, are tribes and people like the others, 'having no hope, and without God in the world.' In all these populous nations, the blessed Saviour, and life and salvation through his name, are unknown. Not a single missionary of the cross is there; and the people are sitting in the region and shadow of death. In view of this entire destitution of the bread of life, what Christian, in his daily prayer of 'Thy kingdom come,' will not bear before the mercy-seat the youth now under a course of Christian instruction, in the very centre of these regions, thus covered with the pall of death. Oh, for the time! when the Church will 'with one accord' plead for those blessings, without which all will be in vain. But to assist in thus training up a native ministry, and above all to preach the Gospel, whom will the Committee send to say to them, 'Behold the Lamb of God, that taketh away the sins of the world'? And where are the individuals and the churches, who will support those now waiting, and the others who, from time to time, are offering themselves willingly to this blessed work?"

Thus it appears that the Mission in Northern India occupies four stations, viz.:

1. LODIANA.—Rev. John Newton, Rev. Henry R. Wilson, Jr., Mr. Joseph Porter, Mr. Reese Morris, Jr., and their wives. The Rev. John C. Lowrie, on a visit to the United States.

At this station is the High-school, in a state of much promise, containing fifty-eight scholars; a female boarding-school just commencing; and a printing-press, with fonts of English, Persian, and Gurmukhi type. As this is at present their principal station in Northern India, the Rev. Henry R. Wilson, Jr., and Mr. Reese Morris, Jr., printer and book-binder, who have recently left the United States, are to be stationed there, with the large printing-press now in India.

2. SABATHU.—Rev. James Wilson, Mr. Wm. S. Rogers, and their wives.

Mrs. Wilson has an interesting school of Gurkha girls. It is uncertain that they will continue their attendance; so far the prospect is encouraging.

3. SAHARUNPUR.—Rev. James R. Campbell, Rev. Joseph Caldwell, Mr. Jesse M. Jamieson, and their wives.

At this station is a boarding and common school, supported by the Juvenile Missionary Society of the First Reformed Presbyterian Church in Philadelphia. Mr. Campbell is a minister in connection with the Reformed Presbyterian Church.

4. ALLAHABAD.—Rev. James McEwen, Rev. John H. Morrison, Mr. James Craig, and their wives.

As this is an important station, the Rev. John H. Morrison, and Mr. James Craig, who have recently sailed for India, were instructed to join it.

At this station is a large boarding-school, which, for want of funds, the Executive Committee were obliged to reduce to twenty scholars. A printing-press will be wanted there the ensuing year.

Mr. Craig is a member of the Reformed Presbyterian Church, as is also the Rev. Joseph Caldwell; the whole amount of his outfit, passage to India, and support for one year, have been provided by that church.

[In the company of missionaries who arrived at Calcutta in 1836, was the Rev. James R. Campbell, afterward D.D., with his wife, of the Reformed Presbyterian Church, General Synod. He and two laymen were appointed by special agreement, not between the two churches, but between the societies, the Western and the Reformed, on the same basis as to their missionary relations to the former with that of its other missionaries. Among the leading members of the Reformed Missionary Society in Philadelphia, were the Rev. Dr. T. W. J. Wylie, and the late Mr. George H. Stuart,—the former secretary, the latter treasurer. The former is still minister of the same church, in later years connected with the Presbyterian body; the latter, an elder in the same church, was distinguished as the leader of the Sanitary Commission Service, and as active in all good work—

especially, as was his friend and pastor, in that of missions; both brethren efficient and beloved.

Dr. Campbell was spared for many years of faithful work in India. He was held in honor by all who knew him; he was a warm-hearted and devoted missionary. Other brethren were sent out by this Society in subsequent years, whose names will appear at the date of their appointment, and whose pecuniary support was provided by the same joint arrangement. But Providential changes eventually terminated, or rather rendered simpler, this joint method; and most of the R. P. missionaries became members of the same Presbyteries with their brethren of the Presbyterian Church.

The Rev. James McEwen and his wife were of the company who arrived at Calcutta in 1836. He was ordained by the Presbytery of Philadelphia; his wife was of a well-known and a highly esteemed family in that city. He was a minister of marked ability in the pulpit, and was encouraged in his labors at Allahabad. After two years his health gave way, and he and his consecrated wife returned to this country. His course at home as a pastor was not long afterwards ended by his death.]

MISSION TO THE WESTERN INDIANS. The Synod of Pittsburgh, at their annual meeting in October, 1833, adopted the resolution to sustain The Western Foreign Missionary Society, "in attempting the immediate supply of every unsupplied and accessible tribe of the Western Indian Reservation, with the means of grace"; and they were greatly encouraged in this benevolent purpose, by the favorable disposition of the general government at that period, in regard to the civilization of the aborigines of our country. In execution of the resolution passed by the Synod, the Society, in the following summer, engaged the Rev. William D. Smith, one of the two missionaries then under the direction of the Society, to undertake an exploring mission through the Indian territories west of the Mississippi. He accordingly spent most of the summer in visiting and conferring with the Shawnees, Delawares, Kickapoos, Kansas, Ottawas, Weas, Iowas, and Omawhaws; and the results of his exploration were approved by the Executive Committee. It was finally determined to select the Weas, as the tribe among whom operations should be commenced; and arrangements were made to despatch a mission to that station in the month of November following. Accordingly on the 4th of that month, the Rev. Joseph Kerr and the Rev. Wells Bushnell and their wives, with Miss Nancy Henderson and Miss Martha Boal, were duly organized as a mission family, and shortly after set out for the place of their destination. After experiencing some disasters in their journey, one of which became the accelerating cause of such a state of impaired health, in respect to Miss Boal, as made it necessary to leave her on the way, the missionaries arrived at Independence, a town in the State of Missouri, about forty miles east of the Wea village, on the 21st of December; and they concluded to pass the winter there. They did so, occasionally visiting the Indians and making preparations for the commencement of more regular labors in the spring. They preached to those whom they visited, by an interpreter; and obtained much useful information relative to their state and character. Mr. Henry Bradley, a young man whom the Committee had accepted as an assistant in the agricultural department, was sent on with supplies to the mission, in the spring. The Wea Indians are a small tribe; but they at once manifested a disposition to receive and treat the missionaries with respect and kindness; so that during the first summer and autumn after their location, besides erecting a school-house, finishing their own dwellings, and making preparations to till a small farm, they opened a school for the children of the natives, and collected the Indians for public and social worship, as often as circumstances would permit. Miss Henderson opened and taught an infant Indian school; and Mr. Kerr and his associate prosecuted their respective labors with great diligence. At the formation of a Temperance Society, although at first somewhat discouraged by the reluctance manifested by many of the Weas to give the pledges of total abstinence, they were subsequently agreeably surprised, when two of the tribe, not formerly present, came forward, without solicitation, and requested their names to be entered.

The following extracts are taken from the Fourth Annual Report in 1836:

"The Mission to the Wea Indians is located in the eastern border of the reserved tract allotted to the emigrant Indians; and may be properly said to comprise two stations, about four miles distant from each other. Our excellent missionary, Rev. Joseph Kerr, and Messrs. Lindsay and Bradley, with Mrs. Kerr, Mrs. Lindsay, and Miss Henderson, comprise the present members of the mission. During the last summer, the schools were fuller and better attended than at any former period, and the prospects of usefulness flattering.

"The Weas, though not numerous, are an interesting people, and have uniformly manifested a disposition gratefully to receive instruction; and this mission has, during the last year, enjoyed special tokens of the divine favor. Besides a growing and very encouraging attention to the means of grace on the part of the Indians, and visible improvement in their morals generally, our brethren have been rejoiced to witness the manifestations of the special influences of the Holy Spirit. Early in the last winter, it pleased the All-wise Disposer of events suddenly to remove by death, one of the most promising of the young men of that tribe, under circumstances which gave encouraging evidence to the missionaries of his interest in Christ. More recently, a church has been organized, to which five native converts have been admitted, and fifteen or twenty more are supposed to be the subjects of religious impression. One of the native converts, a man advanced in years, with locks whitened with age, burst into tears, and indeed into loud weeping, as, in the act of receiving the ordinance of Christian baptism, he publicly submitted himself to the authority of Jesus Christ; and these events, taken collectively, seem to have produced a general excitement among the whole of that tribe of Indians; some becoming warmly enlisted in behalf of the mission, and others aroused to resist its progress. Speaking of one of the oldest and most venerable chiefs of that tribe, and in connection with a small prayer-meeting held at the mission-house, Mr. Kerr states, that, after each had led in the devotions, old Kemassa knelt down and offered an apparently fervent supplication in his own language, on the very spot where, one year before, he lay upon the floor in a state of stupid and helpless intoxication. The progress of reformation and of saving conversion to God among these unhappy remnants of our border tribes, must necessarily be connected with many formidable obstacles; and we are not surprised that our missionary brethren, with these pleasing indications of success in their benevolent work, begin also to experience the opposition of the more debased part of the natives whom they are striving to turn to God."

From the Fifth Annual Report in 1837 we take the following quotation:

"The Wea tribe of Indians have greatly profited by the labors bestowed upon them. A church containing ten native members has been formed in the wilderness, and the hearts of the missionaries have been encouraged by thus early seeing the blessing of God on their labors, among this solitary, degraded, and neglected people.

"Since the commencement of the mission, the Rev. Joseph Kerr and his wife have been at this station. The time of Miss Nancy Henderson was divided between the Weas and the Ioways. During the last year the health of Mrs. Kerr was so reduced by sickness, that, in the opinion of her physicians, nothing but a change of residence and climate gave the least hope of recovery. Early in the winter, while her husband remained among the Indians, she returned to her father's. But the change has not restored her health; and owing to her continued illness, Mr. Kerr has been induced to ask a dismission from the service of the Society, which has been granted. He will remain at the station till the reinforcement lately sent out arrives. On the 14th of March Mr. Henry Bradley and his wife, and Mr. James Duncan, left Pittsburgh for the Wea Mission Station. Miss Henderson, who during part of the winter had been on a visit to her sick mother, since deceased, will join them the first suitable opportunity.

THE IOWA MISSION. "The Iowa Mission comprises but one station, established among a considerable division of the tribe of that name, about eighty-five miles from the Weas. It consists at present of Mr. A. Ballard and wife, and Mr. E. M. Sheppard. Two or three schools were sustained during most of the last summer (1834); and when the missionaries have found it impracticable regularly to assemble the children together, they have spent most of each day in going from lodge to lodge through the village, and giving to their pupils in each family their stated lessons, accompanying them with suitable instructions to the parents and other members of the family. The Iowas, like other tribes, have been much addicted to the excessive and ruinous use of ardent spirits. But the mission has already been highly serviceable in arresting the progress and diminishing the evils of this vice; and the missionaries have been a good deal encouraged by the apparent desire on the part of many to be brought to the knowledge of God.

"During the last year, Mr. and Mrs. Ballard have devoted their whole time to the Ioway Indians. Miss Henderson during part of the summer was engaged teaching the children. Great difficulties were experienced on account of the uncertainty of their residence. Under an arrangement made by the government, the Iowas will remove this spring from their present location to the south of the Missouri River, where 400 sections have been assigned to them and the little band of the Sacs of the Missouri, between the great Nemahaw and the northern boundary of the Kickapoos. The mission family have been instructed to accompany them, and as their home is now considered permanent, the difficulties growing out of an uncertain and temporary residence will cease. On the 14th of March Mr. Samuel M. Irvin and his wife left Pittsburgh to occupy the new station with Mr. and Mrs. Ballard.

"From information which they have been enabled to obtain, the Committee believe that the policy of the Board in the establishment of missions among our Western Indians should contemplate a speedy extension of its efforts to those more numerous and distant tribes, which reside near the sources of the Missouri and its tributary waters. Those people are far less debased and contaminated by the borrowed vices and bad example of our frontier settlements. They are comparative strangers to the use of ardent spirits; and many of them, it is understood, are well inclined towards the great objects of missionary effort."

Thus it appears that the mission to the Western Indians consists of two stations; which, by the last statement of the Corresponding Secretary, stand as follows:

1. WEA STATION.—Rev. John Fleming, Mr. James Duncan, Mr. Henry Bradley, and Mrs. Bradley.

The Church at this station consists of twelve native members and a number of others seriously inquiring the way to be saved.

2. IOWA STATION.—Rev. William Hamilton, Mr. Aurey Ballard, Mr. Samuel M. Irvin, and Miss Nancy Henderson.

During the last year this tribe sold their land to the United States, and have received other land in exchange. They have removed and are now settled—permanently, it is expected—at their new home.

MISSION TO SMYRNA. This mission is not at present in operation. It seems proper, however, that the substance of the statement relative to it contained in the last Report of the Society, should be inserted in this sketch. It is contained in the following extract:

"The Rev. Josiah Brewer and Mr. Thomas Brown, a printer, and his wife, as mentioned in the last report, sailed from New York the 28th of March, 1836, and arrived at Smyrna in May following. They took with them a printing-press and a set of book-binder's instruments. During the last winter the Rev. Wm. McCombs and Mr. John McClintock and their wives, were set apart for this field of labor, and expected to sail in the first vessel leaving the United States. When this reinforcement were on the eve of their departure, Mr. Brown was found very unexpectedly to have returned to this country, having left the station without apprising the Committee of his wish or intention to do so. The unauthorized, and as the Committee judged, unnecessary return of Mr. Brown, and his ceasing on this account to be longer connected with them, made some other measures on the part of the Committee necessary, and brought under their review the whole subject of their mission to Asia Minor.

"Their connection with Mr. Brewer was on the condition that some responsible board or association should assume his support, but no such arrangement had been reported to the Committee, or was known to exist. Much dissatisfaction with this connection existed in the minds of many members of the Presbyterian Church, in view of which Mr. Brewer had signified his willingness that his connection with the Society should be dissolved if thought expedient. Under all these circumstances, the Committee, whilst they entertain for Mr. Brewer sincere and Christian regard, and a desire for his success and usefulness in the missionary field, deemed it best and most expedient that the contemplated connection between him and the Western Foreign Missionary Society should be finally abandoned. Though not under their direction, the Committee hope his valuable labors may still be continued in the Mediterranean, and they will always rejoice to hear that his efforts in this important field have been owned and blessed by the Head of the Church.

"It will probably be found expedient to assign one, if not both of the missionaries, who have been prevented from going to Smyrna by the want of funds, to some other field of labor, where the door of usefulness is more open and the call for assistance more pressing."

MISSION TO CHINA.
The remarks in the last, or Fifth Annual Report of the Society, in May, 1837, introductory to the notice of the appointment of this mission, are so important in themselves, and so necessary to be known and appreciated throughout the whole Presbyterian Church at the present time, that it has been determined to quote the whole, although of a length, which, but for the considerations stated, would render it improper to insert them in this sketch. Immediately after announcing the mission to China, the report proceeds as follows:

"This great people—not more remarkable for the extent of their territory and the number of their population than for their entire ignorance of the true God—have of late engaged the thoughts of professing Christians in all parts of our country. The remarkable fact that one-fourth, or perhaps one-third of the human race, read one language, ought long ere now to have called for the exertion of every friend of missions and of the Bible to give to them that blessed Book in numbers somewhat proportionable to the demand. But alas, a few small editions of the Chinese Bible is the entire supply for these hundreds of millions. The missionary and tract societies of our own and other countries have of late years been most usefully employed in furnishing tracts and Scripture histories; but all that has yet been done cannot bear any comparison to what is yet wanted. The impression that China is closed to missionary exertions seems yet to rest like an incubus on the minds of Christians, and to paralyze and throw doubt on every exertion in her behalf. China is closed in some respects, but China is open and waiting for the Gospel in others.

The Government of China, fearful of European politics, and still remembering the intrigues of the agents of the Church of Rome, have forbidden the residence of foreigners within their limits except at one designated point. The Government do not permit even their language to be taught, nor their books to be sold to foreigners. They forbid also the reading of any books brought by foreigners. They permit no schools to be taught by them, nor printing-presses to be established. New edicts make their appearance from time to time, but these prohibitions are of long standing. Notwithstanding these measures, the people of China are anxious to receive our religious, scientific, and historical books; and if, instead of five thousand copies of the Bible, we had half a million, and prudent and qualified men to distribute them, it would not be long before they would be in circulation in the most thickly-settled part of the empire. All the mandarins and all the military officers could not prevent their teeming millions from receiving and reading them. It ill becomes the Church to be discouraged till the missionaries abroad report to them that nothing more can be done. In other respects, China is open and perfectly accessible to missionary labors. In every island in the Eastern Archipelago Chinese emigrants are to be found, mostly residing together; and only men of a right spirit, sustained by the prayers and the contributions of the churches, are wanted to carry to these accessible perishing thousands the bread of life. These emigrants, to a greater or less degree, are connected with the population at home; many are constantly coming and returning, and thus affording facilities and opportunities to disseminate printed books to a great extent. The hundreds of thousands of the Chinese population, engaged in fishing far out of sight of land and in large companies together, ought neither to be overlooked nor neglected. The attempt to supply them with printed or oral instruction might not in all cases be permitted, because they are for the most part accompanied by war-boats. But let the trial be made. It may be found that these very war-boats will be the first to receive the words of life.

"Heretofore the Chinese printing has been almost entirely performed in the Chinese manner, on blocks of wood. The preparation of these blocks requires the employment of Chinese artists. Hence, nothing could be done without their assistance. The Chinese language has no alphabet, every character represents either a word or an idea. Their number is estimated by Dr. Marshman at 30,000. The expense of preparing steel punches and matrices for such a number would be so great, that, till lately, no attempt has been made to supply the whole. Besides the expense, the difficulty of arranging 30,000 different characters in a printing-office, so as to be manageable by the printer, is seen at once to be too great for practical purposes. The Rev. Mr. Dyer at Penang has been for some time engaged with good success in preparing steel punches and matrices for two or three thousand of the characters most in use. These types when prepared can be used in the common printing-press, and even that number of characters will afford great facility in Chinese printing. Still, it is most desirable that when the missionaries have acquired a full knowledge of the language, they should have the advantage of using any character in it they might prefer in translating or explaining the Bible or in writing their other publications. This most important discovery has quite lately been made. More than thirty years ago Dr. Marshman discovered that most of the Chinese characters consisted of two elements, which he called *formatives* and *primitives*. He pointed out this principle to the student of the language with great clearness, as one of great importance for him to know. Dr. Marshman does not seem to have been aware how very important this discovery was in relation to the preparation of a body of metal type for the whole language. Pursuing the subject with the light thus afforded by this venerable and able missionary, the Chinese scholars in Paris carried it one step further, in reference solely to printing. They divided the whole language into two classes of *divisible* and *indivisible* characters, and by a careful examination of the divisible characters, and a reduction of them to their most simple elements, it appeared that, with 9,000 punches and matrices, the whole 30,000 characters can be formed. By arranging and numbering these 9,000 elements under their respective keys, the whole presents but little more difficulty than a common English printing-office.

"The Committee are much indebted to the Rev. Robert Baird, now in Paris, for the promptitude and ability with which he answered all their letters in relation to this subject. He also forwarded specimens of the printing, which in beauty of form and perfection of finish, excel any Chinese printing with which they have yet been compared in this country. An experienced typographer has engaged to furnish matrices for the whole, or for part of the language, as individuals or societies may order. Deeming the subject of the first importance, in reference to the present condition of China, the Committee, in October last, ordered a set of matrices for the whole language, and forwarded $500 in part payment. The expense at first was stated to be nearly $5,000, but by later information from Mr. Baird, some additional charges for polishing, preparing, and numbering the matrices, amounting to $1,600, must be added. The payment of this additional sum has been assumed by a single individual, which, in the present state of their funds, very much relieved the Committee. There is also some uncertainty whether the whole number of matrices will be made. The typographer states, that for less than two orders, he cannot afford the expense of completing the whole set. No other Society, either in Europe or the United States, has ordered a full set; but the last advices are favorable to a second order being given by the Royal Printing Establishment of France. A number, however, that will be of essential service will be obtained, some of which are already made. With some delay, the whole of the remainder can be furnished by American artists at a small increase of expense.

"The Committee had previously decided to send a mission to China, as large and efficient as the means placed in their hands would justify. For this mission there have been designated two ordained ministers, one physician, and one printer. If the means were afforded, these brethren would in a few weeks be on their way. At present there are not means to send them forward; but the Committee hope the delay will be short; they trust the time is nearly past when the Presbyterian Church will continue to stand with her arms folded, while the millions of China are perishing in her sight."

The writer greatly rejoices that he is able to state, that the Rev. John A. Mitchell, and the Rev. R. W. Orr, and Mrs. Orr, forming an incipient mission to China, sailed for the port of their destination in December last (1837). A physician is delayed for the want of means to send him out. The matrices for the Chinese metal types are in preparation at Paris, with much promise of complete success.

CHINESE
TYPES.
[The Chinese metallic type question had a remarkable history, partly given in the preceding pages. A few lines supplemental may here be in good place.

When the question of ordering a set of the matrices from the artist in Paris came before the Presbyterian Board, it had no missions in China, though one was projected, and two missionaries were under appointment; the expense was estimated at about $6,000; the Board's income was still but small; the request called for faith, especially in view of the declinature by other public and missionary institutions to subscribe in aid of such an experiment. It is not surprising that the new Board should hesitate to incur so large a pecuniary outlay for so apparently doubtful an object.

But looking back a few years, it was deemed singular by the younger members of his family that the Secretary, then in the full measure of public official service in Washington, should decide to rise two hours earlier each morning in order to study Chinese! But this he continued to do for a few years, until, with the aid of dictionary and grammar, he could translate some Chinese books, as well as in a degree to understand matters connected with the language. It was of special interest that this study enabled him to see the *practicable* side of this new type question; and that he had been called by Providence to a post of duty, where he had to consider its missionary bearing. It was finally decided favorably by the Board, partly out of deference to the Secretary's views, and still more owing to the noble liberality of one of the Board's members—the late Mr. James Lenox, who had carefully studied the subject with the Secretary. The order was given; arrangements were made, involving much subsequent patient labor by printers and other missionaries—all ending in complete success. This press is now and has been for years in full work. The Holy Scriptures and other books are printed in electrotype editions. It has become the largest printing establishment in Eastern Asia. It is already securing the confidence of the Chinese, the most conservative people in the world. Their compositors and pressmen are its workmen. Their capitalists and business men, with their energy and industry, and with the lower wages from lower cost of living, will eventually be ready to supersede foreign enterprise—much to the relief of Missionary Boards.]

PROJECTED OR PROSPECTIVE MISSIONS. The Institution, whose missions have now been noticed, is still in its infancy. Those who conducted its operations before it was received under the patronage of the General Assembly, as well as those who now manage its concerns, have been obliged to do what they found to be practicable, and to forego much, very much, that they felt to be desirable. Often it was difficult, as they could do but little, to say who, among the multitude hastening to perdition, they would first attempt to save. The heathen nations were spread out before them, like men perishing by a mighty shipwreck, and as their little relief bark could only go to one here, and another there, the question was embarrassing, what individuals of the sinking throng they would immediately strive to rescue. Hence in their report they point to so many fields of usefulness which they saw it to be desirable, yet found it to be impracticable, to essay to enter, till their means should be greatly enlarged. In their report on their Northern India and China missions, they point to regions of heathen desolation, which all the missions now in action throughout the world, would but very partially supply.

Beside what they there say, toward the close of their last report, they give a distinct article which they entitle "ADDITIONAL MISSIONS," and then add:

"In view of the amount of means that might be contributed by the churches connected with the Society, the Committee believed it to be their duty, to bring into view other stations, which ought to be occupied. Two of these would be, the enlargement of missionary operations among the Indian tribes, another a mission to Calcutta, and another a mission to China." This report, it will be recollected, was made, while as yet the mission, since gone to China, could not proceed for want of the necessary funds. The same want still renders it very imperfect.

INDIAN TRIBES In their last report the Committee say: "Beyond the limits of the respective States, and east of the Rocky Mountains, are forty tribes of various sizes, containing a population of near 200,000. Ten other tribes, or parts of tribes, east of the Mississippi river, with a population of 50,000, are under treaty stipulations to remove west of that river; thus making an aggregate of 250,000, all more or less accessible to the labors of the missionary.

"The Indian territory, as designated by the commissioners to apportion it among the different tribes, is bounded by Red river on the south, and the Missouri and Platte rivers on the north; and is estimated to contain 206,738 square miles—a country more than three times the size of the six New England States, and more than four times the size of Pennsylvania. Upwards of 45,000 Indians have already emigrated to this territory, which, with 6,500 Kansas and Osages residing there, and 50,000, under treaty stipulations to remove within its limits, will make a population of more than 100,000.

Here are no interferences with the jurisdiction or rights of any of the States; and the whole Indian territory will be held by them, under the solemn guarantee of the Government of the United States. In every treaty, the most ample provision has been made for the support of schools, and for teaching agriculture and the most simple of the mechanic arts. It is a most important question, will this experiment of the government, in thus providing a permanent home, save the remnants of this noble race, from the melancholy destiny of those who have perished before the advance of the white man? Is it practicable to elevate the mass of this population, so that in time they may safely be entrusted with all the rights of citizens, and be brought into the Union, on an equal footing with the original States? It would not be difficult to prove, that if the proper means are used, both these questions may be safely answered in the affirmative. But leaving this discussion as not properly belonging to this report, the Committee would notice but one aspect of the question. This experiment will fail most certainly, unless the Indians are made acquainted with the Gospel of Jesus Christ. How important then is the agency the Church has to perform; and how great will be her guilt, if from apathy the part assigned to her is left undone, and thereby all the other efforts fail! In view of this responsibility, the Committee have decided, that as soon as they can obtain qualified men, and the means are afforded, to occupy suitable stations in the Indian territory, and thus to aid in sending the Gospel to every tribe and people within its limits.

"The Committee had also in contemplation to send a mission to the Mandan Indians. They reside high up on the Missouri, and have a population of 15,000. There are many considerations in favor of a station so remote from the white population on the borders of the settlements. There are also disadvantages. The Committee are not prepared at present to occupy this station; and this mission must wait till the spirit of the churches has reached a higher elevation in favor of foreign missions. In the meantime the Committee will seek for the best information in relation to all the tribes upon our borders.

MISSION TO CALCUTTA. "Looking to our large and extending missionary establishments in Upper India, the Committee have decided to establish a mission at Calcutta. Through this place all the remittances and supplies for the upper stations must be sent. This city is the seat of the British Government in India. It is crowded and surrounded by a heathen population; and the devoted laborers from other societies now there, are anxiously looking to this country for assistance in this arduous work.

"The Committee have not definitely selected any other stations in India. What additional points they may be able to occupy, will depend on the men and the means which may be at their disposal. A pressing call has been made in favor of Munipore, a station about half way between Calcutta and Ava, and on the direct road between the two cities. Various stations on the Ganges above Benares are very eligible, and call loudly on the churches to occupy them. It is the wish of the Committee, as soon as practicable, to make arrangements for occupying one or more stations, at or above Allahabad, the station now occupied by a part of the last missionaries sent to India. All these stations would be on the direct travelling road from Calcutta to Lodiana."

[The purpose of establishing a mission at Calcutta

was not fulfilled, partly because that city ceased to be the chief business port of the missions in the upper provinces. The steamers superseded the sailing vessels; the railroads, the bulgerows and tents; the bills of exchange, the recoinage of American half-dollars into Hindu rupees;—changes gradually taking effect soon after the statement above was published, resulted in more convenient methods of missionary business. In some respects Bombay became the mission's port. But the principal reasons for the proposed new mission were lessened in force by the greater number of missionary laborers, foreign and native, who in a few years made Calcutta their centre of work.

Besides, one of the younger men, just fairly entered on the ministry, who possessed extraordinary gifts, which would no doubt have placed him on the principal evangelistic committees in the capital of India, was led to remain at work for Christ in this country—a work largely available also for the missions abroad. All parties cordially concurred in this decision, until at his early end of life, he was eminent above most men in intellect; eminent also in linguistic and especially in Biblical studies, in commentaries—see his work on the two volumes, Earlier and Later, of the prophecies of Isaiah, in which he leaves "the higher critics," so called, with little ground to stand on; indeed, those two volumes ought long ago to have ended controversy on the subject. He wrote commentaries on the Gospel of Mark and the Acts of the Apostles, besides many lectures and review articles. He was remarkable as a preacher of the Gospel, filling the largest churches to overflowing, when it was known that he was to preach; he was certainly one of the most eminent among men of gifts and scholarship, and he was equally remarkable as a modest, humble, devoted servant of the Lord Jesus, even unto the end. The Church has had but few such highly endowed men in its service. It is a privilege to bear one's testimony to such a man, in times of uncertain scholarship. But in this place, he is particularly referred to as ready to be a missionary, and Calcutta was in view by the Board for his field of labor. We can now see more clearly that God gave Dr. J. Addison Alexander the right place for his service.]

THE FOREIGN MISSIONARY CHRONICLE. This publication was commenced by the Western Foreign Missionary Society in the second year (1833) of its existence, and has been regularly continued ever since. It consisted at first of a single sheet, but is now extended to two sheets; and is printed in a very handsome style, and great care is taken to distribute it regularly. No Presbyterian family ought to be without this publication, whatever be the number or character of the other publications which it receives. The price is only one dollar per annum, with a most liberal allowance to agents. A very particular attention is due to the following statement, which appeared on the cover of the January number of the present year (1838):

"At the meeting of the Board of Foreign Missions in Baltimore, it was decided that the *Foreign Missionary Chronicle* should be enlarged. It is important that our churches should be able to take an intelligent interest in the proceedings of our own Missionary brethren, and to offer appropriate prayers to God in their behalf; and it is, also, desirable that every Christian should form comprehensive views of the progress of the kingdom of Christ in the world. Our narrow limits have, heretofore, restricted the amount of information in regard to these objects, which we have desired to communicate. In future, we hope to give our readers a particular account of the proceedings of the Board of Foreign Missions of the Presbyterian Church, and a general view of the transactions of other benevolent institutions; with occasional original communications; biographical sketches of persons engaged in missionary duty, and of converted heathens; notices of books relating to missions; and such other general information as may be adapted to interest the minds of intelligent and reflecting readers. We wish to make the *Foreign Missionary Chronicle* so far a perfect Missionary work, that those persons whose means will not justify them in taking more than one periodical of this kind, and those also whose duties will not permit them to read more than one, will alike find this Magazine adapted to their wishes.

"The *Chronicle* will continue to be published under the direction of the Executive Committee. We are well aware of the difficulty of conducting a work of this kind, in such a way as to meet the views and wishes of all classes of its readers. The outline presented above, describes the manner in which we wish to have it conducted. We hope that it will prove a useful auxiliary to clergymen, and to individual Christians, who wish to co-operate with the Board of their own Church in this sacred cause. It may perhaps become the best, and yet the least expensive agent, which the Board could employ among the churches.

"May we not hope, therefore, to receive the kind countenance of Christian friends, in sustaining and extending the circulation of this work? To the ministers of our churches we respectfully suggest the propriety of recommending it to their people from the pulpit, and on other occasions. We know that, commonly, the degree of interest which any people manifest in the subject of missions, is in precise proportion to the missionary intelligence which they possess. We would, also, solicit the assistance of all who are friendly to this Board, in procuring additional subscribers to the *Chronicle*. Its circulation might, we suppose, at once be increased many thousands; and the present seems to be the most suitable time, for making efforts to secure for it a support worthy of the Presbyterian Church, and of the cause in whose service it is employed."

[The *Foreign Missionary Chronicle* was probably the first periodical of chiefly foreign missions published in the Presbyterian Church of this country. It was edited mainly by the Rev. Dr. E. P. Swift, Corresponding Secretary, and published under the direction of the Executive Committee, at Pittsburgh, Penn., its first number being dated April, 1833. In the next year the services of the venerable and greatly esteemed Rev. John Andrews, who was justly claimed to be the first publisher of a weekly religious newspaper in this country, were obtained to aid in the duties of the mission office, and he rendered valuable aid in editing this publication. On the transfer of the Society to New York, the *Chronicle* was edited for some years by one of the assistant secretaries. In 1850, it was merged in the *Home and Foreign Record*, as the organ of all the Boards. The *Record* was discontinued in 1886, and succeeded by the *Church at Home and Abroad*.

It is worthy of note that, at its first meeting, in 1802, the Synod of Pittsburgh appointed twelve of its members as editors of a magazine,—three of them in special charge. Two large volumes were published in 1803-1805, the *Western Missionary Magazine*, in octavo. They contain valuable articles of religious instruction, selected missionary information, and often quite interesting letters from missionaries of the Synod. The editors do not appear to have received compensation for their labors, but the sum of $334.32 was paid to the mission treasury from its profits. Though references were made in the Synod as to its continuance, no positive information as to a later volume seems to be available.

COLLECTING AGENTS. The W. F. M. Society departed widely from the example referred to on a previous page of the Synodical Commissions, in efforts to obtain funds for its work. The Commissions relied chiefly on the evangelistic piety of their ministers and people; the Society appointed not a few agents to make collections —pastors, unemployed ministers, licentiate preachers, and missionaries under appointment; usually for short periods, and on moderate compensation. In the circumstances then existing this policy was considered expedient by many, though not by all, and after the Society was merged in the General Assembly, it was continued for some years. Its plan was modified, however, so that the services of ministers of large acceptableness were sought, for much larger districts of the country. For a time a General Agent or Field Secretary was in service; then one for two or three States in the East, another for several in the West, etc. It was found difficult to get such men, and more difficult to keep them. Moreover, the true theory of gifts in aid of church evangelizing work was gaining approval—that such gifts are the fruits of divine grace, and are to be sought in the use of the ordinary means of grace. This view of the subject transferred the responsibility of seeking these gifts from the missionary office to the church session and its ministers—very greatly to the advantage of the work. In connection with this, in still later years, the General

Assembly's Committee on Systematic Benevolence rendered valuable service, though in such a Church and in such a ministry as the Presbyterian it would seem that this kind of agency ought not to be long needed.

Keeping to the record, in 1855 all Collecting or Field Agency was discontinued by the Board, and for many years its sole reliance was on the churches. During these years, the two financial crises of the Board's history occurred—one in 1861, when about one-third of its income was withdrawn by the Southern churches, with but little offset for less expenses, most of the missionaries having remained with the Board; the other, a few years later, by the depreciated currency of the country. In both these cases it was the ministers and people who saved the cause. Visiting agents would have been of little use.]

TRANSFER OF THE WESTERN FOREIGN MISSIONARY SOCIETY.

IT only remains to trace the proceeding which resulted in the transfer of the Western Foreign Missionary Society, from the Board of Directors deriving their authority from the Synod of Pittsburgh, to the Board of Foreign Missions of the Presbyterian Church, constituted by the General Assembly of that Church in the United States.

The Convention which met at Pittsburgh in May, 1835, on the recommendation of the signers of the Act and Testimony, issued after the rising of the General Assembly of the preceding year, was the first public body that adopted any decisive measures on this subject. The Act of the Convention referred to, was expressed in the following resolution:

"*Resolved*, That the Committee on the memorial be instructed to present to the General Assembly the solemn conviction of this Convention, that the Presbyterian Church owes it as a sacred duty to her glorified Head, to yield a far more exemplary obedience (and that in her distinctive character as a Church) to the command which He gave at His ascension into Heaven: 'Go ye into all the world, and preach the Gospel to every creature.' It is believed to be among the causes of the frowns of the great Head of the Church, which are now resting on our beloved Zion, in the declension of vital piety and the disorders and divisions that distract us, that we have done so little—comparatively nothing—in our distinctive character as a Church of Christ, to send the Gospel to the heathen, the Jews, and the Mohammedans. It is regarded as of vital importance to the welfare of our Church, that foreign as well as domestic missions should be more zealously prosecuted, and more liberally patronized; and that, as a nucleus of foreign missionary effort and operation, the Western Foreign Missionary Society should receive the countenance, as it appears to us to merit the confidence, of those who cherish an attachment to the doctrines and order of the Church to which we belong."

"After some discussion the above document was committed to the Rev. Drs. Blythe, Cuyler, and Witherspoon, with instructions to introduce the subject to the notice of the General Assembly, through the Committee on Bills and Overtures."

Agreeably to their appointment, the Committee on the Memorial of the Convention presented the foregoing resolution to the General Assembly of 1835. The action of the Assembly on the subject, is contained in the following extracts from their records:

"The Committee on Overture, No. 24, reported and their report was accepted and adopted, and is as follows, viz.:

"The Committee on the papers submitted to them in relation to the Western Foreign Missionary Society, recommend the adoption of the following resolutions, viz.:

"I. That it is the solemn conviction of this General Assembly that the Presbyterian Church owes it, as a sacred duty to her glorified Head, to yield a far more exemplary obedience, and that in her distinctive character as a church, to the command which He gave at His ascension into Heaven: 'Go ye into all the world and preach the Gospel to every creature.' It is believed to be among the causes of the frowns of the great Head of the Church, which are now resting on our beloved Zion, in the declension of vital piety and the disorders and divisions that distract us, that we have done so little —comparatively nothing—in our distinctive character as a Church of Christ, to send the Gospel to the heathen, the Jews, and the Mohammedans. It is regarded as of vital importance to the welfare of our Church, that foreign as well as domestic missions should be more zealously prosecuted, and more liberally patronized; and that as a nucleus of foreign missionary effort and operation, the Western Foreign Missionary Society should receive the countenance, as it appears to us to merit the confidence, of those who cherish an attachment to the doctrines and order of the Church to which we belong.

" II. *Resolved*, That a committee be appointed to confer with the Synod of Pittsburgh, on the subject of a transfer of the supervision of the Western Foreign Missionary Society, now under the direction of that Synod; to ascertain the terms on which such transfer can be made, to devise and digest a plan of conducting foreign missions under the direction of the General Assembly of the Presbyterian Church, and report the whole to the next General Assembly.

"Dr. Cuyler, Dr. Cummins, Dr. Hoge, Dr. Witherspoon, and Dr. Edgar were appointed this Committee."

On the second day after adopting the foregoing report of their Committee, the General Assembly passed the following resolution:

"*Resolved*, That the Committee appointed to confer with the Synod of Pittsburgh, on the subject of a transfer of the supervision of the Western Foreign Missionary Society to the General Assembly, be authorized, if they shall approve of the said transfer, to ratify and confirm the same with the said Synod, and report the same to the next General Assembly."

The Committee appointed by this resolution made to the General Assembly of 1836 the following report:

"The Committee appointed by the last Assembly, on the transfer of the Western Foreign Missionary Society to the General Assembly, made a report, which was read and accepted, and is as follows, viz.:

"The Committee appointed under the following resolution of the last General Assembly, viz.:

"'*Resolved*, That the Committee appointed to confer with the Synod of Pittsburgh, on the subject of a transfer of the supervision of the Western Foreign Missionary Society to the General Assembly, be authorized, if they shall approve of the said transfer, to ratify and confirm the same with the said Synod, and report the same to the next General Assembly,' beg leave to report —That they submitted the following terms of agreement to the Synod of Pittsburgh, at its sessions last fall, and that it was duly ratified by that body, as will fully appear by its minutes.

"Terms of agreement between the Committee of the General Assembly and the Synod of Pittsburgh, in reference to the transfer of the Western Foreign Missionary Society.

"1. The General Assembly will assume the supervision and control of the Western Foreign Missionary Society, from and after the next annual meeting of said Assembly, and will thereafter superintend and conduct, by its own proper authority, the work of foreign missions of the Presbyterian Church, by a Board especially appointed for that purpose, and directly amenable to said Assembly. And the Synod of Pittsburgh does hereby transfer to that body, all its supervision and control over the missions and operations of the Western Foreign Society, from and after the adoption of this minute; and authorizes and directs said Society to perform every act necessary to complete said transfer, when the Assembly shall have appointed its Board; it being expressly understood, that the said Assembly will never hereafter alienate or transfer to any other judicatory or board whatever, the direct supervision and management of the said missions, or those which may hereafter be established by the Board of the General Assembly.

"2. The General Assembly shall, at its next meeting, choose forty ministers and forty laymen, and annually thereafter ten ministers and ten laymen, as members of the Board of Foreign Missions, whose term of office shall be four years; and these forty ministers and forty laymen, so appointed, shall constitute a board, to be styled 'The Board of Foreign Missions of the Presbyterian Church in the United States'; to which, for the time being, shall be entrusted, with such directions and instructions as may from time to time be given, the superintendence of the foreign missionary operations of the Presbyterian Church; who shall make annually to the General Assembly a report of their proceedings; and submit for its approval such plans and measures as may be deemed useful and necessary. Until the transfer shall have been completed, the business shall be conducted by the Western Foreign Missionary Society.

"3. The board of directors shall hold a meeting annually, at some convenient time during the sessions of the General Assembly, at which it shall appoint a president, a vice-president, a corresponding secretary, a recording secretary, a treasurer, general agents, and an executive committee, to serve for the ensuing year. It shall belong to the Board to receive and dispose of their annual report, and present a statement of their proceedings to the General Assembly. It shall be the duty of the board of directors to meet for the transaction of business as often as may be expedient, due notice of every special meeting being given to every member of the board. It is recommended to the board to hold, in different parts of the Church, at least one public meeting annually, to promote and diffuse a livelier interest in the foreign missionary cause.

"4. To the executive committee, consisting of not more than seven members, besides the corresponding secretary and treasurer, shall belong the duty of appointing all missionaries and missionary agents, except those otherwise provided for; of designating their fields of labor, receiving the reports of the corresponding secretary, and giving him needful directions in reference to all matters of business and correspondence entrusted to him; to authorize all appropriations and expenditures of money; and to take the particular direction and management of the foreign missionary work, subject to the revision of the board of directors. The executive committee shall meet at least once a month, and oftener if necessary; of whom three members, meeting at the time and place of adjournment or special call, shall constitute a quorum. The committee shall have power to fill their own vacancies, if any occur during a recess of the board.

"5. All property, houses, lands, tenements, and permanent funds, belonging to the Board of Foreign Missions to be constituted by this agreement, shall be taken in the name of the Trustees of the General Assembly, and held in trust by them, for the use and benefit of the Board of Foreign Missions for the time being.

"6. The seat of the operations of the Board shall be designated by the General Assembly.

"After some discussion, the above report was committed to Dr. Phillips, Mr. Scovel, Dr. Skinner, Dr. Dunlap, and Mr. Ewing, who were authorized to review the whole case, and present it for the consideration of this Assembly.

"*Resolved*, That the report of this committee be the order of the day for Thursday morning at 10 o'clock, or earlier if prepared."

The committee appointed at the close of the foregoing minute, made the following report:

"The committee to whom was referred the report of the committee on the transfer of the Western Foreign Missionary Society, and an overture on the same subject from the Synod of Philadelphia, made a report, which was accepted, and is as follows:

"The committee to whom was referred the report of the committee appointed by the last Assembly, on the subject of a transfer of the supervision of the Western Foreign Missionary Society to the General Assembly, and also the overture from the Synod of Philadelphia, on the subject of foreign missions, report—That the attention of the last Assembly was called to the subject of foreign missions by the following overture, viz., on page 31 of printed minutes:"

The committee here recite what was done in the preceding year, as already stated, and which need not be repeated. They then continue in their report as follows:

"Thus it appears, that the proposition to confer with the Synod, and to assume the supervision and control of the Western Foreign Missionary Society, originated in the Assembly.

"At that time the Western Foreign Missionary Society was in a prosperous condition, enjoying the confidence and receiving the patronage of a considerable number of our churches, having in their employ about twenty missionaries, and their funds were unembarrassed. The committee having conferred with some of the members of that Society, and finding that the proposition was favorably regarded by them, indulging the hope that an arrangement might be definitely made with the Synod at their next stated meeting, by which the Assembly would be prepared to enter on the work at their present sessions, brought the subject again before the Assembly, when it was, after mature deliberation,

"'*Resolved*, That the committee appointed to confer with the Synod of Pittsburgh, on the subject of a transfer of the supervision of the Western Foreign Missionary Society to the General Assembly, be authorized, if they shall approve of the said transfer, to ratify and confirm the same with the said Synod, and report the same to the next Assembly,'—p. 33.

"The committee thus appointed, and clothed with full powers to ratify and confirm a transfer, submitted the terms on which they were willing to accept it, to the Synod of Pittsburgh, at their sessions last fall.

"The members of the committee not being present at the meeting of the Synod, and there being no time for further correspondence, the Synod (although they would have preferred some alterations of the terms) were precluded from proposing any, on the ground that such alteration would vitiate the whole proceedings, and therefore acceded to the terms of the transfer which were proposed by the committee of the Assembly, and solemnly ratified the contract on their part. Feeling themselves bound by the same, and trusting to the good faith of this body, they have acted accordingly, and have made no provision for their missionaries now in the field for a longer time than the meeting of this Assembly, having informed them of the transfer which has taken place, and of the new relation they would sustain to this body after their present sessions.

"It appears then to your committee, that the Assembly have entered into a solemn compact with the Synod of Pittsburgh, and that there remains but one righteous course to pursue, which is to adopt the report of the committee appointed last year, and to appoint a Foreign Missionary Board. To pause now, or to annul the doings of the last Assembly in this matter, would be obviously a violation of contract, a breach of trust, and a departure from that good faith which should be sacredly kept between man and man, and especially between Christian societies—conduct which would be utterly unworthy of this venerable body, and highly injurious to the Western Foreign Missionary Society.

"The committee beg leave further respectfully to remind the Assembly, that a large proportion of our churches (being Presbyterians from conviction and preference) feel it to be consistent not only, but their solemn duty in the sight of God, to impart to others the same good, and in the same form of it which they enjoy themselves, and to be represented in heathen lands by missionaries of their own denomination. They greatly prefer such an organization as this contemplated, and which shall be under the care of the Presbyterian Church, and cannot be enlisted so well in the great and glorious work of sending the Gospel to the Heathen, under any other. Already, with the blessing of the great Head of the Church on the efforts of the Western Foreign Missionary Society in this form of operation, has a missionary spirit been awakened among them to a considerable extent, and an interest in the cause of missions been created, never before felt by them. They have furnished men for the work, and are contributing cheerfully to their support in the foreign field.

"As one great end to be accomplished by all who love the Redeemer, is to awaken and cherish a missionary spirit, and to enlist all the churches in the work of evangelizing the world; as every leading Christian denomination in the world has its own foreign missionary board, and has found such distinct organization the most effectual method of interesting the churches under their care, in this great subject; as such an organization cannot interfere with the rights or operations of any other similar organization, for the field is the world, and is wide enough for all to cultivate; as it is neither desired nor intended to dictate to any in this matter, but simply to give an opportunity of sending the Gospel to the heathen, by their own missionaries, to those who prefer this mode of doing so, giving them that liberty which they cheerfully accord to others—your committee cannot suppose for a moment that this General Assembly will, in this stage of the proceedings, refuse to consummate this arrangement with the Synod of Pittsburgh, and thus prevent so many churches under their care from supporting their missionaries, in their own way. From this view of the case, they recommend to the Assembly the adoption of the following resolutions, viz.:

"1. *Resolved*, That the report of the committee appointed by the last Assembly, to confer with the Synod of Pittsburgh, on the subject of a transfer of the Western Foreign Missionary Society to the General Assembly, be adopted, and that said transfer be accepted, on the terms of agreement therein contained.

"2. *Resolved*, That the Assembly will proceed to appoint a Foreign Missionary Board, the seat of whose operations shall be in the city of New York.

"The above report was made the order of the day for to-morrow morning at 9 o'clock."

The discussion in the General Assembly on this important concern was much protracted. The parties were very nearly equal in numbers, and on both sides deeply interested. The following are the dates and minutes, exhibited in the record of the proceedings had on the subject:

"Thursday morning, May 26, 1836.—The Assembly, agreeably to the order of the day, took up the report of the Committee to whom was referred the report of the Committee of the last Assembly, on the transfer of the Western Foreign Missionary Society.

"Dr. Skinner, one of the Committee, who dissented from this report, made a counter report, which was read, accepted, and is as follows:

"Whereas, the American Board of Commissioners for Foreign Missions has been connected with the Presbyterian Church from the year of its incorporation, by the very elements of its existence; and whereas, at the present time, the majority of the whole of that Board are Presbyterians; and whereas, as it is undesirable, in conducting the work of foreign missions, that there should be any collision at home or abroad; therefore,

"*Resolved*, That it is inexpedient that the Assembly should organize a separate Foreign Missionary Institution.

"A motion was made to adopt the report of the Committee; after considerable discussion, a motion was made to postpone the motion for adoption of the Committee's report, with a view to take up the report of

Dr. Skinner. While this motion was under discussion, the Assembly adjourned till this afternoon at half-past 2 o'clock.

"Thursday afternoon, May 26th.—The Assembly resumed the unfinished business of this morning, viz., the postponement of the motion for the adoption of the report of the Committee on the transfer of the Western Foreign Missionary Society; after considerable time spent on the subject, the further consideration of it was suspended, to give an opportunity to the Committee appointed to count the votes for members of the Board of Missions, to report.

"The Assembly resumed the subject of the transfer of the Western Foreign Missionary Society, and it was further discussed.

"Friday morning, May 27th.—The Assembly resumed the consideration of the unfinished business of last evening, viz., the transfer of the Western Foreign Missionary Society. The forenoon was spent in the discussion of this subject.

"Friday afternoon, May 27th.—The unfinished business of the morning, viz., the transfer of the Western Foreign Missionary Society, was resumed; and after considerable discussion, the question was taken on the motion to postpone the motion for adopting the report of the Committee, to take up the report of Dr. Skinner, and was decided in the negative. The yeas on this motion were 133, and the nays 134."

Thus it appears, that on this question the members of the Assembly in favor of the transfer, had a majority of a single vote. After this, the subject was not again called up, till Thursday morning, the 9th of June, when the final vote was taken; the record of which is as follows:

"The report of the Committee on the transfer of the Western Foreign Missionary Society, was taken up, and after considerable discussion, the previous question was moved and carried, when the main question on adopting the report, to transfer the Western Foreign Missionary Society to the General Assembly, was put, and was decided in the negative, as follows: yeas, 106; nays, 110."

Thus, in a body of 216 voters, it was decided by a majority of four votes, to set aside a formal solemn contract, entered into with the Synod of Pittsburgh, under the sanction of the General Assembly of 1835; and to refuse the acceptance of the transfer which the Synod had actually made, on the faith that the contract to which they had been invited, would certainly be fulfilled. A very able protest, with 87 signatures, was entered against this proceeding; and was answered, or rather replied to, by a Committee of the majority of the Assembly, appointed for the purpose. These papers are too long for insertion in this sketch; and after the quotations already made, are not necessary to a full understanding of the views and aims of the disagreeing parties. . . . .

[The author's report of these events refers to some things that were omitted in the narrative, presumably as already known to readers of that day. Complete information, however, is still readily accessible, in the Minutes of the General Assembly of the years 1835, 1836, and 1837, in which the various resolutions, amendments, substitutes, votes, protests, and answers to protests,—in short, the full proceedings can be found of record. The Annual Reports of the Western Foreign Missionary Society, in 1836 and 1837, should also be referred to,—see particularly, page 33, of the Report of

1837; and the Circular Letter of the Board of Directors of the Society, of June 26, 1836.

The adverse action of the Assembly on the transfer was viewed as threatening disaster to the Society. A conference was held in Philadelphia early in June, 1836, by its friends and patrons, including members of the Assembly, Directors of the Society, and others, when it was agreed that a statement of the case should be made by the Directors, in the form of a Circular Letter. This letter was written by Dr. Elisha P. Swift, Corresponding Secretary, and submitted to the Executive Committee, under date of June 27, 1836. It is worthy of his great ability, suitable to the grave responsibilities of the situation, and admirable in its Christian spirit. It is here inserted in full.

"DEAR BRETHREN: It devolves upon us, by the appointment of the Board of Directors of the Western Foreign Missionary Society, to address you in its behalf, under circumstances of unanticipated and extraordinary embarrassment.

"The General Assembly of 1835, as you are doubtless aware, appointed a Committee, to treat with the Synod of Pittsburgh on the subject of the transfer of the Society, with all its missions and its funds, to the supreme judicatory of our Church; and authorized and empowered that Committee, if they could obtain terms which to them appeared satisfactory, to ratify and confirm a contract to that effect. At the last annual meeting of the Synod, that Committee submitted, with an authentic certification of their appointment and of their plenary powers, certain propositions and articles to which they were prepared, in the name of the Assembly, to accede; and which required the virtual relinquishment by the Synod, from and after its assent to them, of all jurisdiction over the Society and its operations. The existing Board, by the joint authority of the Assembly's Committee and the Synod, was to continue its superintendence until a new Board should be appointed. The Synod, impressed with the belief that there were interspersed through various parts of the Presbyterian Church, a large number of our body by whom an ecclesiastical organization for foreign missions was earnestly desired; and whose zeal, energy, and affectionate co-operation, in the work of sending the Gospel to the Heathen, could be secured only by such a plan; and sensible that no one Synod could properly claim the right to direct the operations of an important branch of Christian enterprise in which many others were equally interested, and which they were expected to sustain, came to the determination, after protracted and prayerful deliberation, to accept the overtures of the Assembly; and did forthwith, as all parties fully understand the act, fulfil the only remaining condition of the contract.

"To the Synod, as they were invited to form an arrangement in which their missionaries abroad and their churches at home were deeply interested, the inquiry naturally enough arose, whether the Church, by her General Assembly of one year, could bind herself in a contract which would be, in its essential principles, beyond the control of her Assemblies of other years; and whether she could do that by her agents which she had power to do herself. It need hardly be said, that these questions admitted of but one answer. The acts of the Church, by her General Assembly, like those in the case of any other representative body, assume different forms, according to the subjects to which they refer. When they belong to the class of contracts involving pecuniary considerations and the rights of others, as where the Assembly accepts donations and bequests, to be used or held in trust for particular objects, the irrepealable obligation of the engagement is apparent to every mind, and is recognized in every court of justice. The second inquiry admitted, if possible, a still more obvious solution than the first, as the General Assembly, by its Trustees and Boards of Direction, was every year making bargains and executing trusts not less permanent or responsible than that which was now contemplated. The Synod, therefore, in good faith, entered into an engagement, which it was foreseen would in the meantime necessarily occasion a serious interruption of business, and eventually prove a heavy pecuniary loss to the Society, if the operations were not promptly carried forward by the Assembly. As the Society was sustaining no unpropitious missions, and was possessed of funds far beyond all present demand, the Board did not look upon it as an act of condescension on the part of the Church, to adopt the Society as its own; and as the Board had uniformly maintained towards their fellow-laborers of the American Board the most amicable relations, they did not think of giving offense, even to its most ardent friends in the communion of our Church, by co-operating in an arrangement which could only put the advocates of ecclesiastical organization on a par with their brethren, while it would obviously increase the amount of good to be achieved.

"The General Assembly, as you have doubtless heard, after a protracted discussion, resolved not to fulfil the provisions of this arrangement, nor receive the Society which had thus been transferred to them. When that portion of the Board of Directors, who were then present in Pittsburgh, found the missionary operations of the Society thus left unprovided for, and themselves without the opportunity of consultation with the Synod, they resumed their deliberations, and adopted a resolution inviting those members of the Assembly who had voted for the transfer to unite in an expression of their views as to the course proper to be pursued. Such a meeting was accordingly convened, and resolutions were unanimously passed, recommending to the Board to resume its functions; expressing it as the sense of the meeting, that every one then present should use his influence within the bounds of his respective Presbytery to make the condition and the wants of the Western Foreign Missionary Society known to the churches, and obtain for it all possible funds, both from contributions at the monthly concert, and in other ways, to be paid over to the treasurer of each Presbytery, and by him transmitted to the Treasurer of the Board—'That, in resuming the work of missions, the Western Foreign Missionary Society is hereby assured of our confidence and zealous co-operation; and that where suitable agents cannot be obtained to visit the churches we will encourage the members of our Presbyteries to undertake voluntary agencies for the benefit of the same.'

"As the decision of the General Assembly may possibly be thought to have originated in some objection to the Society itself, or the character of its missionaries, and may thus be construed to its disadvantage in its future operations, it may be proper to say, that, with the exception of one of the speakers, who animadverted with some severity upon the Committee for having received, as a missionary under its care, a brother not in connection with the Presbyterian Church, nothing was said which could justly impeach the credit of the Society before the Christian public. It was indeed urged against its adoption by the supreme judicatory of our Church:

"1. That it might involve us in collision with the American Board, and produce division and strife; but it was not alleged that the Society had, in past years, incurred this imputation; nor was it shown that Christian candor and fairness required the Church to oppose an ecclesiastical Board on this ground, while it unhesitatingly encouraged a voluntary one; in other words, that this difficulty, if it should prove one, ought to annihilate our institution only, while it encouraged and supported that of our Congregational brethren.

"2. It was said, that, if the sanction of the General Assembly were given to a Board of Foreign Missions, that board might claim, on its authority, the aid and co-operation of such parts of the Church as desired to give their support to the American Board; but it was not shown that a refusal to countenance such a board at all, might not be equally construed to mean that the Assembly expected all its Presbyteries and churches to patronize that institution; nor was it shown that the other Boards of the Assembly have ever been able to make such a use of their authority.

"3. It was urged, that it should be the purpose of all Christians, in sending the Gospel to the heathen, to lay aside all denominational peculiarities, and present Christianity to the heathen only in those aspects in which the opinions of all evangelical believers agree. But the same brother, who so eloquently urged this theory, did, in a previous argument, on the same subject, attempt to show that the American Board was more of a Presbyterian than a Congregational institution; and consequently liable to the same objections which were preferred against ours. The argument itself, if just, would have gone as truly to subvert all existing missionary boards as to oppose the reception of ours, since no one of them pretends to act upon the principle which it sustained.

"4. It was urged (and these four comprise the principal objections which were mentioned in the debate) that the reception of the Board under the care of the Assembly would be inconsistent with pledges already given to the American Board; and, at least, it would imply a want of confidence in the wisest and best conducted missionary institution on earth. But those who supported the measure, and some who opposed it, denied the propriety of pursuing any such course of reasoning. Thus, without going further into particulars, it will be seen that the Assembly did not profess to have discovered in the character or operations of this Society any thing which should induce its former friends to withdraw from it; nor should the course and issue of a discussion, in which its constituted officers took no part, array the prejudices of any portion of the community against it.

"Of the decision of the Assembly itself we forbear to speak. For the majority in this case we entertain great respect, as brethren and fellow-laborers in the service of our Lord. We attentively listened to most of the discussion, and we have since carefully, and we hope candidly and prayerfully, weighed the reasons embodied in their answer to the protest of the minority; and we confess our surprise that, on grounds to us so insufficient, they should have thought it their duty to suppress, by efforts so strenuous and by a majority so small (110 to 106), a plan which could hardly fail to insure a more universal diffusion of the spirit of foreign missions, and to promote, in the present excited state of our Church, a feeling of harmony among its members. What if the preceding Assembly had been indiscreet, and had conferred upon its committee 'unwarrantable and improper powers'? It does not invalidate a contract, that it was prematurely or unwisely entered into (Psalm xv. 4) nor does it prove that the object itself is inexpedient. What if a majority of the last Assembly preferred a voluntary to an ecclesiastical organization, their concurrence in the adoption of the Society involved no sacrifice of opinion, and left them at full liberty formally to decline all co-operation with any but the American Board. Nor is this all. The constitution of the Presbyterian Church manifestly contains the presumption, that operations of this kind are to be carried on church-wise (Form of Gov., chap. 18), and consequently presents the impossibility of securing a general ecclesiastical organization, but through the General Assembly. Now when almost all the larger denominations of evangelical Christians both in Europe and America, including the Church of Scotland from which we derive our origin, have adopted the ecclesiastical form of foreign missionary operation, it is hard to see how a conscientious member of a Presbyterian Assembly, bound by his ordination vows to study the prosperity of *that church*, should feel himself required to prohibit that church from embodying its yet unapplied strength in the most important of Christian efforts. That, in a course to us so unexpected, our brethren sincerely intended to glorify God, and promote the salvation of a perishing world, we would not deny; but, it is our persuasion, that, on cool reflection, they will find occasion to regret that the influence of excited feeling on other and irrelevant questions, has unduly obtruded itself into one which makes a solemn claim to separate and dispassionate consideration. In the present state of our Church, could such a decision be expected to increase the amount of effort for benighted lands? In so far as it disappoints the wishes of probably at least one-half of the Presbyterian Church, it should be met with the candor, meekness, and charity which become the followers of Christ, at all times, and which especially befits this sacred enterprise.

"In the course of argument pursued in the Assembly, there was one point which we seem required to notice. Portions of letters from one of the Secretaries of the American Board, recently published, were read in the debate to show that the Presbyterian Church 'had no occasion to withdraw its confidence' in the wisdom and fidelity of that Board; and it was generally understood that these letters were intended to bear upon the decision which the Assembly were expected to make of the question of the appointment of the new Board. Whether this was strictly proper after the committee had given its pledge to the Synod in the name of the Assembly we will not pretend to say. Our only object is to say in reference to this matter, that it is certainly doing injustice to the friends of this measure, to suppose that their preference of an ecclesiastical arrangement implies any such want of confidence. It would certainly be deemed unkind to impute to our Congregational brethren, motives like this, when they exhibit their preferences. So far as good men are persuaded to believe that such an intention is cherished by us, as a Society for Foreign Missions, they may be expected to withhold their sympathies and their prayers from us; and, as we are now required to go on with our labors, it stands us in hand to fortify ourselves against every injurious prejudice. We may then confidently say that we have, as individuals and as a Board, never published a word that could, by fair construction, be made to express the slightest suspicion of this kind. This Society has indeed held out to such as preferred our form of operation to the other an invitation to co-operate in sending the Gospel to the heathen; but it has spoken of the American Board in the highest terms of respect and confidence. To assume it, therefore, as true that all desire for another and an ecclesiastical Board, must imply a want of confidence in that, and then go on to reason against the measure as though it were intended to create and sustain suspicion and disturb the tranquillity and confidence of the churches, must appear to every candid mind to be unintentionally fostering the very spirit which it professes to condemn. We should have passed this fact in silence, if it had not awakened in us a desire to guard, if possible, against future misunderstanding. In our first Circular Address to the churches, published early in 1833, will be found the following remarks: 'In reference to the American Board of Commissioners for Foreign Missions we hope to cherish no selfish principle, and we shall appeal to no sectarian feeling. We do contemplate its past achievements and its present prosperity with unmingled pleasure. Our only strife will be, to copy its every good example, and try not to be outdone by it in kind affection and Christian magnanimity. We hope to be able, as a Presbyterian Board (perhaps in a feeble and humble measure), to increase the amount of missionary feeling and effort in our Church; but certainly, on such principles of mutual harmony and brotherly co-operation as every sincere disciple of Christ will desire to witness' (*Missionary Chronicle*, April, 1833, p. 6). But if the very existence of a Presbyterian Board—if any separate attempt to 'increase the amount of missionary feeling and effort in our Church,' must be construed to imply a want of confidence in the American Board, and a defection in what is due to that organization, it would be a hopeless matter in our future operations, as it would seem to have been in the past, to prosecute our work with 'mutual harmony and brotherly co-operation.' Our only alternative would be to abandon the work altogether, and forever deprive the perishing heathen of that amount of good which hundreds of churches might be expected to yield if they had a Board of their own election. We desire now to proceed on the same principles with which we commenced. And as we prize harmony and good feeling, and mutual co-operation in the work of the Lord, above almost everything else, and have no desire whatever to involve this great enterprise with any collateral controversy in the Church, we object to the idea altogether, that our present and future existence should be held up to the churches in this light. And, if a future General Assembly should be willing to own us among its real friends, we hope and pray that it may never be thought or said that it cannot be done without a breach of good faith to that excellent Board, and the excitement of suspicion as to its wisdom and fidelity. We wish to do the work which they cannot do; but we also wish and pray that they may grow and prosper more and more in the affections of all good men.

"The fact, that of the two decisions which the last Assembly (to say nothing of the preceding one) had on this question, at different periods, one was for and the other against, the proposed measure, is sufficient evidence that the operations of neither can be safely suppressed. In this broad land where churches multiply by hundreds every year, and the resources of religious men by thousands; and which, ere long, must send its missionaries by hundreds annually to the four quarters of the globe, who will pretend to say, that there should be but one channel, and all ecclesiastical preferences should be suppressed, in order to the accomplishment of this end? Which would be the most evangelical liberality, to attempt to bring all denominational differences to bend to this, and curb and fetter their action until they should, or to urge one and all of them to be up and doing, to hasten the great consummation with all their might; and to do this with the expectation that all hurtful prejudices would gradually vanish away, as the great work would grow upon their hand, and nation after nation come forth into the light and liberty of the Christian redemption? Is it a matter of doubt to any candid observer, whether the foreign missionary operations of the Methodist Episcopal Church, as such; the American Baptist Church, as such; and the Protestant Episcopal Church, as such; are destined to exert a benign influence upon the entire character of these respectable denominations? Could there be any prospect of, or would there be any utility in, their consenting to drop all their respective peculiarities, and unite in one association whose principles should comprise no one distinctive feature of either? Would they ever come together by being required to wait until they could thus agree, and, in the meantime, leave the entire heathen world to perish in their sins? Why then should it be thought or represented as sectarian—as unworthy of our character as liberal-minded Christians, to desire to see the Presbyterian Church, as such, organized and embodied in this great and precious service?

"In view, then, of the circumstances in which we are now

placed as a Society, and a Church, by the aspect of the world—by the example of sister denominations—and by the decision of the last General Assembly, let us, beloved brethren, arise with new energy and zeal, to prosecute the too-much neglected work of foreign missions. Let not the disappointment of our plans, and the unexpected counteraction of our reasonable wishes, fill our minds or the souls of our people with discouragement and despair. If our eye is single—if our intentions are sincere, we can present the pressure of our circumstances before the throne of God with increased confidence. Our brethren, who, by such immense exertions, were barely able, after several of our friends had left their posts, to vote down the contract, will, on reflection, see how impossible it is for us to secure a general ecclesiastical organization but through the General Assembly, and they will become convinced that nothing can be gained to them, much less to the cause of foreign missions, by attempting to prevent it; throwing upon themselves, as it must, a great amount of responsibility, and giving no additional acceptability to the Board for whose sake they propose to do it. If we are active, and prompt, and prayerful, in the cause; if we bring the foreign missionary enterprise before the minds of our people, and before God, with a growing conviction of its importance, Heaven will listen to our supplications, and the Redeemer of Israel will provide. A question like this will lose nothing by standing on its own naked merits before the Church and the world ; and our Church will, in due time, award to us with little opposition, that organization which it would have been undesirable to gain by a bare majority.

"In the meantime, the Board of the Synod will resume its duties and go forward, relying upon the pledge of active co-operation given by the brethren from all parts of the Church, in the meeting to which we have referred. From the spirit of that meeting, they hope and trust it may be a year of great results. In the provision of missionaries and assistant missionaries, as well as in the collection of funds, and the diffusion of missionary intelligence, much aid may be rendered to the Executive Committee by individual ministers, and by Presbyteries in all parts of the Church ; and thus aided, the Board hope to keep pace with the growing energies of the churches. We affectionately entreat our brethren in the ministry, in the eldership, and in the communion of the Church, to come up to the help of the Lord ; and countenance, with their contributions, their prayers, and their best energies, the attempt which must now be made to secure such an organization and concentration of effort in this work as these eventful times require. Our Church has surely strength and vigor enough to throw off the obstructions which oppress her, and take her place among those sister denominations by whose ecclesiastical appointment the trumpet of the Gospel is sounding in Burmah, in Africa, in Greece, and the wilds of America. In the former, what conquests over a dark and cruel superstition have our Baptist brethren begun to realize, and what trophies of their piety and zeal are our Methodist brethren endeavoring to rear up on the shores of paganism ? Unawakened by these and other examples, is our body to sit still, or to append its contributions to another institution, and never make its voice distinctly heard in the great and eventful day of the conversion of the nations ? This enterprise is God's and not man's ; and every Christian, and every denomination, must expect to forfeit the richest influences of His grace, if there be neglect and defection when the chief Captain of the hosts marshals His forces for the day of His power. Ye watchmen of Israel ! what of the night ? Are not the circumstances of the world eventful ? Are they not such as to show that all our Sabbath-schools should be nurseries of the missionary spirit ? that our monthly concerts should be replenished with the spirit of grace and supplication, and that all our judicatories and churches, in hope, in zeal, and activity, be as those who wait for the coming of the Lord? Surely then our Church will arise, and not remain inactive, to wait for the realization of a beautiful theory of missions, or for fear that she may offend others by fulfilling the command of Christ herself. May the God of missions pour out His Spirit upon us—raise up many devoted, heroic missionaries for the work, and cause the blessing of many ready to perish to come upon us! Amen."

FINAL MINUTES OF THE WESTERN FOREIGN MISSIONARY SOCIETY. Between the meetings of the General Assemblies of 1836 and 1837, the friends of the Western Society gave time, reflection, and prayer to the subject of their Christian duty. The Assembly's adverse action was taken by so small a majority as not to settle the question; it was doubtful from the two votes of the Assembly whether the majority was really adverse. But the question involved such important principles and such grave issues, that the Society's supporters felt constrained to go forward, notwithstanding serious discouragements. Still maintaining the organization of their Missions under Church direction and supervision, they were led to decide on two changes, both looking to more general and efficient measures. One was to substitute *Presbyterian* for *Western* in the name, and the other to remove the seat of operations to the city of New York—all parties consenting.

Following the *dates of events*, the last Minutes of the Society, printed as an Appendix by the author, are here inserted. They were adopted prior to the Assembly's proceedings of 1837, but at the usual time when the Annual Meeting of the Society was held. They show that its purpose was onward, by the blessing of God.]

"Philadelphia, May 23, 1837.

"Agreeably to the Constitution of the Western Foreign Missionary Society, the Annual Meeting of the Board of Directors was held in the session room of the Sixth Presbyterian Church, Philadelphia, on Tuesday, May 23, 1837, at half-past 7 o'clock, P.M."

The names of the members of the Board, and of the Directors of the Society, are then given in detail. It appears that there had been appointed, five representatives of the Synod of Pittsburgh, and six of the Synod of Philadelphia. The Presbyteries of Alleghany, Blairsville, Carlisle, Erie, Kaskaskia, Louisville, Miami, New Castle, Philadelphia, Philadelphia 2d, Redstone, Sidney, and Susquehanna, had also each appointed representatives, agreeably to a provision of the Constitution; of whom twenty-six were present. The minutes continue as follows:

"Rev. Dr. Green, Vice-President, opened the meeting with prayer.

"The following resolution, submitted by the Corresponding Secretary, Mr. Lowrie, after full deliberation, was decided in the affirmative:

"*Resolved*, That the interests of the Missionary cause, as connected with the Western Foreign Missionary Society, require a change of location of the centre of its operations from the city of Pittsburgh."

With two exceptions, all the members present voted for this resolution. The minutes then proceed as follows:

"The Rev. David Elliot, D.D., and the Rev. T. D. Baird, being members of the Executive Committee, after the above members had voted, expressed their acquiescence in the above vote in the affirmative.

"*Nays*—none.

"The constitution of the Society requires, that to

carry the affirmative of the above question, there be a majority in the affirmative of all the members of the Board existing at the time; and there being 26 votes out of the 35, the resolution was adopted.

"The following resolution was then submitted, viz.:

"*Resolved*, That the centre of operations of the Society be, for the present, in the city of New York.

"After an interchange of sentiment till a late hour, the Board adjourned till half-past 8 o'clock to-morrow.

"WEDNESDAY, May 24, 1837.

"The Board met pursuant to adjournment, and was opened with prayer by the Rev. Dr. Elliot.

"The consideration of the unfinished business was resumed, and after full deliberation, was decided in the affirmative.

"The Corresponding Secretary laid before the Board the following paper, which had been read by him on yesterday:

"'In order to facilitate the plan of the contemplated removal of the centre of the operations of the Western Foreign Missionary Society, and to provide for the organization of an Executive Committee, in the place to which the said centre may be removed, we, the undersigned, members of the Board, do hereby resign our seats in the same, that our places may be filled, at the annual meeting of the Board, with persons residing near the future location of the Society.

'FRANCIS HERRON.
'ROBERT PATTERSON.
'E. P. SWIFT.
'JOHN HANNEN.
'SAMUEL THOMPSON.
'ALEXANDER SEMPLE.
'ALEXANDER LAUGHLIN.

'PITTSBURGH, April 24, 1837.'

"On motion,

"*Resolved*, That the above vacancies in the Board of Directors be filled with the following named persons:

"Rev. W. W. Phillips, D.D.   Rev. E. W. Crane.
  "   Joseph McElroy, D.D.   Mr. James Lenox.
  "   John M. Krebs.   " James Paton.
  "   Nicholas Murray.

"*Resolved further*, That the above named persons be appointed members of the Executive Committee; and that Alexander Symington, Esq., be the President of the Society, the Rev. Ashbel Green, D.D., Vice-President, and Mr. James Paton, Treasurer.

"On motion,

"*Resolved*, That the name and style of the Society be 'THE PRESBYTERIAN FOREIGN MISSIONARY SOCIETY.'

"On motion,

"*Resolved*, That the Rev. Francis Herron, D.D., Rev. David Elliot, D.D., Rev. T. D. Baird, Rev. E. P. Swift, D.D., Rev. John Nevin, Rev. Robert Patterson, Walter H. Lowrie, Samuel Thompson, Alexander Semple, John Hannen, and Alexander Laughlin, of the city of Pittsburgh and vicinity, be a Board of Agency for the Presbyterian Foreign Missionary Society, for the Western States; with such powers as may be necessary to aid the Executive Committee in the appointment of Agents for bringing out the resources of the churches in the Western States, and for conducting the missionary operations among the Indian tribes.

"Adjourned to meet on Friday, the 26th instant, at half-past 7 o'clock, P.M., in the Central Presbyterian Church.

"Friday Evening, May 26, 1837.

"The Board met pursuant to adjournment, at the Central Presbyterian Church. This being the evening appointed for the public Anniversary of the Society, a large assembly being present, the Rev. James Blythe, D.D., opened the meeting with prayer.

"Extracts of the annual report were read by the Corresponding Secretary.

"Addresses were then made by the Rev. Archibald Alexander, D.D., Rev. R. J. Breckinridge, Rev. John A. Mitchell, and the Rev. Wm. S. Plumer; and, at a late hour, the congregation was dismissed.

"The Board continuing in session, on motion by the Rev. Dr. Cuyler,

"*Resolved*, That the Annual Report be adopted, and that it be published and distributed under the direction of the Executive Committee.

"*Resolved*, That the Rev. George Potts and Moses Allen, Esq., be appointed members of the Board, in the room of the Rev. David Elliot, D.D., and the Rev. T. D. Baird, resigned, and that Mr. Allen be a member of the Executive Committee.

"Adjourned to meet in Baltimore, the last Friday in October next."

The Board of the Western, now the Presbyterian, Foreign Missionary Society, held its last meeting in Baltimore at the time specified in the foregoing adjournment; but did no business, except that which related to the transfer of all its concerns, to the Board of Foreign Missions of the Presbyterian Church in the United States of America. Communications had been received from the Synods of Pittsburgh and Philadelphia, the former of which had passed, and the latter had subsequently adopted, the two following resolutions:

"*Resolved*, 1st, That the Board of Directors of the Presbyterian Foreign Missionary Society, in so far as they derive authority from us, be and they hereby are empowered and directed to transfer to the Board of Foreign Missions of the General Assembly, to meet in the city of Baltimore on the 31st instant, the said Society, with all its funds, Missions, and papers.

"*Resolved*, 2d, That the members of the said Board of the Presbyterian Foreign Missionary Society, now acting in the same by virtue of appointments made by this Synod, be authorized and appointed to act, from and after this date, so long as may be necessary duly and properly to execute the said transfer, and no longer, at which time the said Board shall be considered as dissolved."

The foregoing resolutions were passed by the Synod of Pittsburgh on the 26th of October, and by the Synod of Philadelphia on the 30th of the same month, 1837. On the day after the last mentioned date, the following paper was laid before the Board of Foreign Missions, viz. :

"We, the undersigned, members of the Board of Directors of the Presbyterian Foreign Missionary Society, deriving our authority from the Synod of Pittsburgh, in pursuance of the direction of the said Synod, in their resolution of the 26th October, 1837, do hereby transfer to the Board of Foreign Missions of the Presbyterian Church, the said Society, with all its funds, Missions, and papers. It being understood, that this transfer shall not in any manner affect or annul the principles on which the missionaries now under the care of the Presbyterian Foreign Missionary Society, from the Reformed Presbyterian Church, were received; but the said missionaries shall sustain the same relation to the Board of Foreign Missions of the General Assembly, which they have sustained to the Presbyterian Foreign Missionary Society.

"WALTER LOWRIE.
"WILLIAM W. PHILLIPS.
"NICHOLAS MURRAY.
"JAMES LENOX.
"JOHN M. KREBS.

"BALTIMORE, October 31, 1837."

FINAL ACTION OF THE GENERAL ASSEMBLY.

IN the same year, A.D. 1837, the following transactions took place. This Minute embodies the Constitution of the Board of Foreign Missions of the Presbyterian Church in the United States of America.

"Wednesday Morning, June 7, 1837: The Committee on Overture No. 7, viz.: the overture from the Presbytery of Salem, on the subject of foreign missions, made a report, which was accepted, and adopted, by yeas and nays, as follows, viz.:

"1. *Resolved*, That the General Assembly will superintend and conduct, by its own proper authority, the work of Foreign Missions of the Presbyterian Church, by a Board appointed for that purpose, and directly amenable to said Assembly.

"2. The General Assembly shall at its present meeting, choose forty ministers and forty laymen, as members of the Board of Foreign Missions, one-fourth part of whom shall go out annually, in alphabetical order; and thereafter ten ministers and ten laymen shall be annually elected as members of the Board of Foreign Missions, whose term of office shall be four years; and these forty ministers and forty laymen, so appointed, shall constitute a Board to be styled, 'The Board of Foreign Missions of the Presbyterian Church in the United States of America,' to which, for the time being, shall be intrusted, with such directions and instructions as may from time to time be given by the General Assembly, the superintendence of the foreign missionary operations of the Presbyterian Church. This Board shall make annually to the General Assembly a report of their proceedings, and submit for its approval such plans and measures as may be deemed useful and necessary.

"3. The Board of Directors shall hold their first meeting at such time and place as may be directed by the present General Assembly, and shall hold a meeting annually, at some convenient time during the sessions of the General Assembly, at which it shall appoint a President, Vice-President, a Corresponding Secretary, a Treasurer, and an Executive Committee, to serve for the ensuing year. It shall belong to the Board of Directors to review and decide upon all the doings of the Executive Committee; to receive and dispose of their annual report, and to present a statement of their proceedings to the General Assembly. It shall be their duty, also, to meet for the transaction of business as often as may be expedient, due notice of every special meeting being seasonably given to every member of the Board.

"4. To the Executive Committee, consisting of not more than nine members beside the Corresponding Secretary and the Treasurer, shall belong the duty of appointing all missionaries and agents; of designating their fields of labor; receiving the reports of the Corresponding Secretary, and giving him needful directions in reference to all matters of business and correspondence intrusted to him; to authorize all appropriations and expenditures of money; and to take the particular direction and management of the foreign missionary work, subject to the revision and control of the Board of Directors. The Executive Committee shall meet at least once a month, and oftener if necessary; five members, meeting at the time and place of adjournment or special call, shall constitute a quorum. The committee shall have power to fill their own vacancies, if any occur during the recess of the Board of Directors.

"5. All property, houses, lands, tenements, and permanent funds, belonging to the said Board of Foreign Missions, shall be taken in the name of the Trustees of the General Assembly, and held in trust by them for the use and benefit of 'The Board of Foreign Missions of the Presbyterian Church in the United States of America,' for the time being.

"6. The seat of operations of the Board of Directors shall be designated by the Board.

"7. The Board of Directors shall have power, and they are hereby authorized to receive a transfer of the Foreign Missionary Societies, or either of them, now existing in the Presbyterian Church, with all the missions and funds, under the care of and belonging to such societies.—Yeas, 108; Nays, 29.

"Mr. Plumer offered the following resolutions, which were adopted, viz.:

"1. *Resolved*, That a committee be appointed to nominate Directors for the Board of Foreign Missions. The names of ministers and elders as Directors were nominated by the Committee and elected by the General Assembly. [See Minutes G. A., June 7, 1837.]

"2. *Resolved*, That the Board of Foreign Missions be directed to hold their first meeting in the First Presbyterian Church, in the city of Baltimore, on Tuesday, the 31st of October next, at 3 o'clock P.M."

Thus, at length, were the wishes and prayers answered of those who had long and earnestly desired to see a Board of Foreign Missions, under ecclesiastical appointment and responsibility, established in the Presbyterian Church of the United States, acting in its distinctive character.

[The missionary discussions in the General Assembly were now ended. They turned on the question, whether the cause and work of foreign missions should be conducted by the organized Church or by voluntary societies? By the societies was not meant denominational voluntary organizations; these might be expedient when the greater part of the Church was opposed to missions. But the societies referred to were such as were formed by evangelical Christians of all denominations—as at first the London Missionary Society. The Church theory was, and is, in our American sense, both ecclesiastical and denominational in its scope. Church doctrine and Church government have a divinely appointed place in the work of missions.

Men of marked ability had taken opposite sides on this subject, but yet in most cases without unkind feeling. It seems to have been considered apart from discussions of other subjects in the same year. A recent re-perusal of the G. A. Minutes tends to confirm the belief that foreign missionary affairs were considered in a Christian spirit, earnest yet not partisan; in a zeal worthy of the sacred cause. Most Presbyterian people, and many of other denominations, now hold the Church theory; but the particular questions under discussion in those days now awaken little interest. After many years of divided but practical and amicable experience, the Presbyterian Church is now one body in its support of this sacred cause.

The transferred Society brought into the larger field a work that had sprung from right views and motives; a work well begun; free from debt; having an income advancing each year, until at its end it was seven-fold larger than at its beginning—indeed, larger than was then given to foreign missions by all the other churches of the denomination; and, moreover, supporting several existing missions of great promise, with others in preparation. With the blessing of God, this work in its great field has ever since, under the direction of the General Assembly, steadily gained influence, power, and blessed results for earth and heaven—for time and eternity.]

THE POSITION. [This, then, is the position. We hold that the duty of missions is divinely and most clearly revealed, and that the practical measures by which this duty is performed may be, and in ordinary times ought to be, determined by the judicatories of the Church. These judicatories will always embrace many of the most able and experienced men in our communion, and their measures will usually be governed in the long run by the public sentiment of the Church—a public sentiment which every church member contributes to form and has the power to influence. We thus combine conservative and popular principles; the voluntary power of numbers with the safer action of the few, who are yet responsible, while they are clothed with a wholesome authority. Measures, therefore, which, not being expressly revealed, are left to the wisdom and judgment of the Church, in the study of Providence and in answer to prayer, may be safely committed to the supervision of our church courts. This is true of missions as of other things. And the missionary policy which secures their approval, after due consideration and trial, will commend itself to the approbation and the support of the members at large.

On what does the work of Foreign Missions hinge in our Church? We answer, not mainly on questions of missionary policy; we are, for the most part, agreed about them. But the turning point of the whole enterprise is this, that the hearts of the people become interested in the work. And how shall this result be obtained? By dwelling chiefly, we do not say exclusively, but chiefly, on the great truths on which the whole work is founded. Each follower of Christ will feel—" I am commanded by my Lord, by my Redeemer, to give His Gospel to my fellow-men; I am commanded to do this. And if I have the spirit of the Gospel, I will do unto others as I would have them do unto me —have I, then, the spirit of Christ in this matter? Those poor heathens are dying. Can I help to save them? I shall meet them at the judgment-seat of Christ. Will my conscience, will my Judge, then be satisfied with what I am now doing for their salvation? Their eternity will be as long as mine; their souls are worth as much as mine; their time here is as short as mine; their song of praise to redeeming grace would sound as sweetly as mine. What, then, am I doing to put them in possession of the blessed hopes which I enjoy myself? All that I have has been received from God through the blood of Christ. I am not my own. Lord, what wilt Thou have me to do?" These, and such like, are the thoughts and feelings which should fill the hearts of all Christians. Now, what are the considerations which will call these feelings into life and invigorate them? There is but one answer, and that is found in the plain truths of God's Word, and the outpouring of the influences of the Holy Ghost.]

FIRST MEETING OF THE BOARD OF FOREIGN MISSIONS. The Board of Foreign Missions of the Presbyterian Church in the United States of America met in Baltimore, agreeably to the order of the General Assembly, on the 31st day of October, 1837. The Minutes of this meeting were duly recorded and afterward were published in pamphlet form of twelve pages. They are usually bound for reference with the Annual Report of the Board for 1838.

Suitable record was made of the Board's Constitution; acknowledgment was recorded of the action of several Synods, particularly those of Pittsburgh and Philadelphia; and the transfer of the Presbyterian Foreign Missionary Society, as recorded in its Minutes, was accepted by the Board as follows: "*Resolved*, That the transfer of the Presbyterian Foreign Missionary Society to the Board be accepted on the terms and conditions specified; and that the Executive Committee be directed to communicate this fact to the Synods of Pittsburgh and Philadelphia, and to take necessary order on this subject."

The city of New York was unanimously chosen as the principal seat of operations of the Board. Executive officers were elected, viz.: *President*, Rev. Samuel Miller, D.D., Princeton; *Vice-President*, Gen. William McDonald, Baltimore; *Executive Committee*, Rev. William W. Phillips, D.D., Rev. Joseph McElroy, D.D., Rev. John M. Krebs, Rev. George Potts, Rev. Edward D. Smith, Mr. James Lenox, Mr. Moses Allen, Mr. Henry Rankin, and Mr. Hugh Auchincloss; *Corresponding Secretary*, Hon. Walter Lowrie; *Treasurer*, Mr. James Paton. And other preliminary and usual measures were taken for entering with vigor on the work of the Board.

A public religious service was held in the First Presbyterian Church in the evening. And after recording an expression of thanksgiving to God for His great favor to this cause, the Board adjourned, to meet in the Second Presbyterian Church, Philadelphia, on Tuesday after the first Thursday in May next, at 3 o'clock P.M., concluded with prayer.

The Central and the Southern Boards of Foreign Missions, supported respectively by the Synods of Virginia and North Carolina and the Synods of South Carolina and Georgia, were also transferred at this period or a little later to the Board of Foreign Missions of the General Assembly. Their work for a few years had been connected with the American Board; but in accord with the tenor of their relations to that Board, this transfer was cordially made and accepted.

[The adjournment of the Presbyterian Foreign Missionary Society to meet in Baltimore, as mentioned on page 218, *supra*, was made at the request of some members, that two general meetings should be held in each year, one in the city where the General Assembly met, the other in a different city, from year to year. Baltimore was chosen for the first semi-annual meeting. This was known to the members of the General Assembly, and probably led to the order that the "first meeting" of the Board of Foreign Missions should be held in that city, in the First Presbyterian Church. And a meeting of great interest and influence was duly held there. It was a convenient time and place, moreover, and it allowed a few months' delay for necessary legal measures to be completed in placing the Society's now considerable property and its titles in the ownership of the Board.

The policy of holding semi-annual meetings of the Board, after some further trial, was relinquished; for the reason only, that it was found to be difficult, if not impracticable, to hold these fall meetings without inconvenience to the autumnal meetings of Presbyteries and Synods. This precluded the general attendance of ministers and elders at a semi-annual meeting of the Board.]

CONCLUDING REMARKS.

FROM the preceding compendious view of Missions in the Presbyterian Church of the United States, it appears that this Church has not been altogether insensible of the importance of so great and sacred a concern, nor wholly inactive in the discharge of her duty. In domestic missions her exertions have been laudable, and her efficiency considerable; but in heathen and foreign missions, she has reason to mourn over her remissness, and to be humbled in view of her small participation in the great work of evangelizing the world. It is true indeed, that since the revival of the missionary spirit, within the last fifty years, certain unpropitious circumstances, some of which the present sketch has brought into view, have tended to restrain her efforts in foreign missionary enterprise, and to hold her in comparative inaction. But no apology can justify the past neglect; and far less would its continuance admit even of palliation. By the good providence and gracious interposition of God, the Presbyterian Church in this country is, at present, in a situation more favorable than ever heretofore, for commanding all her resources, and exerting her whole strength in propagating the Gospel. The wise and decisive action of the General Assembly of 1837, has delivered her from the paralyzing effect of an unfriendly extraneous influence; and having now her Boards of Education, and of Domestic and Foreign missions, formally and fully established, free from internal as well as external counteraction, she has at her disposal all the necessary means for extensive and effective operations, in the foreign as well as the domestic missionary field. It is now for her to justify or to falsify, the allegation that has often been made by some, not the most friendly to her institutions, that she has neither the zeal nor the skill indispensable for managing effectively a great missionary concern. Every consideration, therefore, both of character and duty, loudly demands from all her children, to put forth their whole force, and to bring into action all their means, to wipe away her reproach, and to give her a vigorous operation in obeying her risen Saviour's parting command to His disciples; and to repair, as far as it can be repaired, her past neglect, and demonstrate that she is animated by a sincere concern for the salvation of souls, and a supreme regard to the glory of God—in a degree not exceeded by any Church in Protestant Christendom. All this, her numbers and her resources put fully in her power, if that power be exerted under the influence of a holy, wisely directed, and well tempered zeal. To contribute to this high object, as far as his ability extends, let the author of the foregoing sketch be permitted, respectfully to submit to his brethren of the Presbyterian Church, some considerations which appear to him to demand a general and very serious attention.

1. The importance of sustaining our missionary operations on right principles, and from right motives. A regard to character has been mentioned; and the commendation which the Apostle Paul bestowed on the churches of Achaia, and his declaration that their example had "provoked very many," shows that this motive may lawfully have a degree of influence. Yet doubtless it ought to be subordinate to one of an infinitely higher order; for if the preservation of character itself be not regarded as subservient to the glory of God and the promotion of His cause in the world, it loses its

chief value. What we want is, that it should be brought home to the heart and conscience of every professing Christian, male and female, in the Presbyterian Church, that there is a palpable defect, a manifest flaw in Christian character, so long as he or she does nothing to send the Gospel to the heathen. Surely the positive command of the Saviour to "preach the Gospel to every creature," either was obligatory only on the apostles, and their successors, the ministers of the Gospel, or else that it was, and still is, binding on all Christians alike, each "according to the ability that God giveth." Suppose then—what is believed not to be the fact—that the command of Christ was intended to be directly obligatory only on the preachers of the Gospel, still the question dictated by inspiration will demand an answer; "how shall they preach except they be sent?" To be sent, implies that he to whom it relates goes on the errand of another; although he may feel a deep interest for himself, in the business of his mission. Professing Christians then, must send the preachers—the missionaries who go to proclaim the Gospel to the heathen. This manifestly involves the duty of qualifying them to be sent, and of supporting them in their missionary work, in such manner as shall enable them to perform it with the greatest efficiency; so that this duty is brought directly back, with all its solemn sanctions, to the bosom of every professing Christian. Here is the true missionary principle; and it is the only principle that can be relied on for the regular, constant, and adequate support of missionary operations. Novelty and a powerful appeal to the feelings, whether of a popular audience or of individuals in private, will frequently produce great temporary effects. But the influence of excitement is always transient, and is often followed by indifference, and sometimes by disgust or aversion. Now, in the missionary concern, we want something that can be calculated upon, as steadily, permanently, and effectively operative—and here we find it. We find it in a deeply settled principle, working on the heart and conscience of every Christian, that he and she are bound by the allegiance and the gratitude they owe to the Saviour, in whom is all their own hope for eternity, to send His soul-saving Gospel to the millions who, for want of it, are perishing in ignorance and sin. If this principle can be radicated in the hearts of Christian professors generally in the Presbyterian Church, we shall never know the want either of funds or of missionaries for heathen missions. Parents, under the divine blessing, will instil the principle into the minds of their children, the young will imbibe it from the old, talented and educated youth will feel its constraining power and covet the missionary work; the widow, too, will bring her mite, the poor man his dollar, and the rich man his hundreds or thousands, and cast them cheerfully into the consecrated treasury. In a word, the Church of God, in her embodied strength, will "come up to the help of the Lord against the mighty." Ministers of the Gospel and elders of churches, therefore, should use incessant efforts to inculcate this principle, in every congregation. "Do you hold this principle and purpose, by the grace of God, to act upon it?" may not improperly be a question propounded to every individual, when application is made for the full communion of the Church.

2. Before the world shall be converted to God, there must be a practical conviction—just such a conviction as some of our best missionaries, now among the heathen, tell us has sunk into the depths of their souls—that it is the power of God alone, working by His Spirit on

the minds of the heathen, that can ever change them
—raise them from the abyss of their depravity and awful degradation, renew them unto holiness, inspire them
with the faith and hope of the Gospel, and prepare
them for communion with God on earth, and the more
perfect communion of the heavenly state. But in close
connection with this full sense of dependence on God
alone for the conversion of the heathen, there will be a
firm and lively faith in God, that in His own good time,
His almighty grace will actually produce this effect, notwithstanding all the wretchedness, abandoned vice, and
almost brutal debasement, in which pagan nations are
now beheld; and notwithstanding all the opposition
which may be made from earth and hell—because He
has promised, and cannot lie, that His beloved Son, as
the reward of His sufferings and death, "shall see of
the travail of his soul and be satisfied," and expressly
"I shall give thee the heathen for thine inheritance, and
the uttermost parts of the earth for thy possession."
Here, in the next place, will be the firm foundation for
the prayer of faith; prayer which will take hold on the
promises of God as divine realities, that must and will
meet their accomplishment; prayer which will plead
for the fulfilment of the divine engagements with an
earnestness like that with which Jacob wrestled with
the angel of the covenant; prayer which will regard
not only the perishing state of the heathen, but which
also will look beyond and above it—look to the triumph
of the Redeemer over the prince of darkness, in the
total subversion of his empire, and the establishment on
its ruins of the kingdom and the reign of Immanuel;
prayer, in a word, that will contemplate the glory of the
blessed God, Father, Son, and Holy Ghost, shining in
all its splendor, when the riches of divine grace are

displayed in the congregated host of the elect, gathered from every kindred and people and tongue under heaven.

Now, as it is believed that there must be a great increase of these things, among Christians in general, before the arrival of the Millennial age, so the more there is of them, in reference to the missionary operations now going on in our own and in other churches, the greater will be the well-founded hope, that these missions will be crowned with a large and the most desirable success. Not only should their best endeavors be used by the judicatories of the church, and by the minister and elders of particular congregations, to secure a better attendance on the monthly concert, and a right management of it when the people convene for its observance; but in country places, and in the winter, it may be expedient to have two or three locations, instead of one, in which the people of a neighborhood may meet in small companies for social prayer, and other exercises appropriate to the stated season of devotion. This will take away most of the ground for the common reason assigned for absence from the concert, that the distance of the church from a large part of the congregation, and the difficulty and even danger of travelling in the dark, prevents a general attendance. It ought also to be inculcated on those who cannot or do not attend, that they may and ought, in their private retirements, to spend some time in special prayer, while their brethren are spending it in social devotion. If this be done with a proper frame of mind, the concert will be observed by those who are absent, as well as by those who are present in a particular place. A prayer-hearing God may be addressed in any place, and those who pray in private, in the manner recommended, may mingle their petitions and their praises with those who assemble for the purpose.

3. Dependence on God for the success of missions to the benighted pagans ought not to diminish, but to increase, the means and exertions that we use to produce this effect. The great encouragement which is presented to us in the oracles of inspiration, to be diligent and persevering in the use of means, is, that they are appointed by God, and, as His ordinary dispensation, indissolubly connected with His blessing. Our Saviour's command to ask, seek, and knock, is connected, as an encouragement, with the declaration that "he that asketh receiveth, and he that seeketh findeth, and to him that knocketh it shall be opened"—and this declaration, or promise, is, by himself, directly applied to the gift of the Holy Spirit. "If ye then being evil, know how to give good gifts to your children, how much more shall your Heavenly Father give the Holy Spirit to them that ask him." In like manner, the apostle Paul enjoins on the Philippians—"Work out your own salvation with fear and trembling"—and why?—"For it is God that worketh in you, both to will and to do, of His good pleasure." Here the entire efficiency and sovereign good pleasure of God, in the matter of our salvation, is assigned as the very reason why we ourselves should work it out—assigned as a powerful encouragement, as it unquestionably is; for what encouragement to use all our own efforts can be so animating, as the knowledge that we have an Almighty Helper to aid us, and whose good pleasure it is to work in us and with us, and to render our faithful endeavors successful.

Among the means for the prosecution of missions, funds and missionaries are at once seen to be essential.

In the foreign field, nothing can be done without them. In addition to what has already been suggested on this topic, let the writer be permitted to express his conviction that there has never yet been, among the professors of religion in the Presbyterian Church, anything like a general and just estimate of the amount of property which each individual ought, as a matter of sacred duty, to dedicate to the Lord. Some few instances of noble Christian liberality have been witnessed; but take the church at large, and probably not one professor of religion in fifty has done all that an enlightened sense of duty would have dictated. It is believed, however, that penuriousness in this matter has been less owing to absolute inherent avarice than to the want of considering the subject seriously and viewing it in a proper light. It cannot be discussed at any length in this sketch, and must be left to be brought before their people by the pastors of our churches. The great point to be carried, as before stated, is to get it fixed in the mind of every professor of religion that there is a sacred duty to be performed in this concern, and an estimate to be made, as in the sight of a heart-searching God, of what each individual ought to give; and then, without unnecessary delay, to give it cheerfully and systematically. The want of system in this concern is one great cause of defect in the amount contributed. When people give only by impulse they think that what (themselves being judges) is a handsome donation, made now and then, not only acquits them of their obligations, but renders them meritorious. Whereas if they would take an account of what the God of providence has put into their hands as His stewards and say, as in view of their last account, what portion of it they ought, annually or habitually, to render back to Him as a voluntary thank-offering, and from a desire to promote the cause and build up the kingdom of their Redeemer in the world, it would reach an amount far beyond what is produced by impulse; and be attended, moreover, by the comfort of an easy mind and an approving conscience.

Generally speaking, missionaries must be young men. The time may come when some men in middle life, or beyond it, may be called to quit places of eminence in the church at home and go on missions. At present we look to the pious, and talented, and educated youth of our churches to devote their lives to this sacred work. When any young convert, under the constraining influence of love to his Redeeming God, thinks of devoting his life to the service of that Redeemer in the Gospel ministry, it might be well, at the present day, if he would immediately put the question to himself whether he is willing to go out as a missionary to the heathen? and, in like manner, young converts of both sexes, who have no prospect or thought of the ministerial vocation, may do well to ask themselves whether, in the stations for which they are, or may be, severally qualified, they are willing to leave all for Christ and to become instruments of making His preciousness, of which they now taste the sweetness, known to the perishing pagans. This would be one good method of bringing the genuineness of their conversion to the test, and of impressing their minds, through the whole of their subsequent lives, with the unspeakable importance of missionary work. But nothing could be more contrary to the opinion of the writer than that all who have no personal reluctance to go, either ought to go, or are fit to go. His judgment is that no occurrence could be more disastrous to the church than a heedless enthusiasm to go out on missions; resembling that of the crusaders, to dispossess the Mohammedan Saracens of the Holy Land. No, verily, while every real convert ought to be unreservedly devoted to the service of God; and while it may be of great use for all to think early, that they may think long, and at last justly, on the subject of missions, yet much meditation, much prayer and fasting, and much attention to the aspect of Providence, and much consultation with the most pious and judicious Christians, should invariably precede the determination of any individual to offer to be a Christian missionary. Many may have much of a true missionary spirit, and yet may not possess that bodily constitution, or those mental qualities, or that freedom from existing ties and engagements, without which it cannot be expedient or lawful to assume the missionary character. When a missionary proves unfaithful and becomes a reproach to the cause, he does it an injury which cannot be calculated; and in the contemplation of which any one who thinks of being a missionary may well tremble. The error, however, at present is commonly found on the side, not of too much, but of too little zeal; and the best means that can be devised ought to be brought into operation to impress the minds of our theological students, whether in the public seminaries or under the direction of private teachers, with the sacred obligations that may be resting on them to give themselves to the Lord for His service in foreign lands. Yet there ought not to be anything that virtually amounts to constraint or compulsion in this matter. For if a missionary's whole will and heart are not set on his work he will be likely to faint and desire to abandon it when he comes to encounter its difficulties and privations. O for a host of Brainerds and Martyns in the Presbyterian

Church to meet its present missionary exigencies! God can raise them up, and let His people entreat Him earnestly for this inestimable blessing.

4. Faithful missionaries ought to be "esteemed very highly in love for their work's sake"; and every kindness should be shown them on departing from our shores, and every reasonable provision be made for their support in foreign lands; and much sympathy ought to be felt and many prayers to be offered for them in the arduous service in which they are employed. Yet they are neither to be idolized nor flattered. The latter, if it do not spoil, may greatly injure them; and the former may provoke God to cut short their days; to show us that no particular instrument is necessary to the execution of His purposes; and that He can form at pleasure such agents as His work requires. One of the kindest things that can be done for missionaries is to make some provision for their widows and children when they are removed by death; and for themselves when sickness or a broken constitution compels them to leave the missionary field. To this important object it is hoped that in due time the requisite regard will be shown.

5. We ought not to calculate that great and speedy success will follow our missionary enterprises. The instruction of ignorant, debased, and vicious heathen must in the nature of things, require considerable time; and after they are instructed God may see meet to put our faith and patience to a prolonged and painful trial; and yet, if we persevere, He may eventually crown a mission, which seemed to be most unpromising, with the most signal success. So it was in the mission that was fitted out, under the most flattering auspices, to the Sandwich Islands. Years on years elapsed without a

single convert being made, and disaster after disaster befell the mission. Yet at last it seemed as if the prophetic interrogatory, " shall a nation be born at once?" was going to be answered affirmatively. An adverse tide has since set in on that mission by the criminal and reproachful conduct of men calling themselves Christians; but the evil is at length abated, if not removed, and most exemplary Christian churches are there established. Something of a similar kind has often happened. It appears by the foregoing sketch that the glorious success which ultimately rewarded the labors of our own Brainerd did not take place till even his faith and hope seemed on the point of extinction. Let us beware, then, of prescribing to a sovereign God. If He grants speedy success to a particular mission, let us receive it with lively and humble thankfulness; and if, in another mission, or in all the missions we send out, He for a time grants no success, but even seems to frown, as He has done on our African mission, let us bow and adore His holy sovereignty; but let us not despond or be impatient—"In due time we shall reap if we faint not."

6. In managing the missionary concerns at home there certainly ought to be as strict an economy in the use of missionary funds as an enlightened regard to the prosperity of the general cause will permit. To waste or misapply these funds would be a species of sacrilege; and the more gratuitous services that are freely offered the better; provided there be a reasonable prospect that such services, should they be accepted, will be really advantageous. But it is not true economy to grudge a reasonable and liberal compensation to those who give up other employments and devote all their time and talents without reservation to the faithful service of the

Society; because without such a compensation the best services, as all experience shows, cannot be secured; nor the real interests of the Society, even in pecuniary matters, be best promoted. Parsimony here is real prodigality. There ought also to be a reasonable confidence cheerfully granted to those who manage the concerns of the Society; because without it they cannot act with the freedom and promptitude which the exigency of affairs may sometimes imperiously demand. On the other hand, the officers of the Society ought to practice no concealment, nor violate any order of the Board, nor fail to take advice, when it can be easily and seasonably obtained. It is most desirable that all seeking of fame, all regard to great worldly emolument, and all craving of office, should be forever eschewed and cautiously guarded against by those who are concerned in the management of missions. There are some trusts and stations of responsibility which those who covet and take pains to obtain are commonly the least fit to hold; and in the sacred missionary cause it may safely be assumed as a general principle that the best men to be entrusted with its precious and often delicate concerns must be sought for before they are found; that is, they will not ordinarily present themselves as candidates for office, but only yield, and often with diffidence and trembling, to the opinions of their brethren. If the management of our missionary affairs ever becomes an object of worldly or secular ambition, rely upon it, *Ichabod* will be inscribed upon them.

Such are the remarks which the author of the foregoing sketch has ventured to submit to his brethren, in terminating one of the last services that he can reasonably hope to render to the Church of Christ.

APPENDICES.

I.

PRESBYTERIAN FOREIGN MISSIONARIES.

Appointed in 1741. Rev. Azariah Horton, *r.* in 1750.
    1742. Rev. David Brainerd, died in 1747.
    1748. Rev. John Brainerd, died in 1780.
    1763. *Rev. Sampson Occum*, an Indian employed for several years among various tribes.
    1803. Rev. Gideon Blackburn.
    1806. Rev. Joseph Badger.

The preceding list is far from complete.

APPOINTED IN 1832 TO 1838 INCLUSIVE.

To Indian Missions:
  Rev. W. Bushnell and his wife, 1833–1835, *r.**
  Rev. Joseph Kerr and his wife, 1833–1837, *r.**
  Rev. John Fleming, 1837–1839, *r.*
  *Mrs. Fleming, 1837–1839.
  Rev. Peter Dougherty and his wife, 1838–1871, *r.*
  *Rev. William Hamilton, 1837–1891.
  *Mrs. Julia McG. Hamilton, 1837–1868.
  Mrs. Hamilton, 1869–1891, *r.*
  Rev. S. M. Irvin and his wife, 1837–1864, *r.**
  Mr. Henry M. Bradley and his wife, 1834–1841, *r.*
  Mr. F. H. Lindsay, 1835–1836, *r.*
  Mr. Elihu M. Shepherd, 1834–1835, *r.*
  Mr. Aurey Ballard and his wife, 1835–1837, *r.*

---

* Died. In the Mission, if * prefixed. After resigning, if * appended.
r. Resigned or returned.

Miss Martha Boal, 1833-1834, r.
Miss Nancy Henderson, 1833-1836, r.*

To *African Missions, Liberia*:
*Rev. Joseph W. Barr, 1832.
Rev. John B. Pinney, 1833-1835, 1839-1840, r.*
*Rev. John Cloud, 1833-1834.
*Rev. Matthew Laird and his wife, 1833-1834.
Mr. James Temple,† 1833-1834, r.
Mr. F. J. C. Finley, 1834-1835, r.
Mr. E. Tytler,† 1837-1839, r.

To *Missions in India*:
*Rev. William Reed, 1833-1834.
Mrs. Harriet Reed, 1833-1835, r.*
Rev. John C. Lowrie, 1833-1838, r.
*Mrs. Louisa A. Lowrie, died in Calcutta, November 21, 1833.
Rev. James Wilson and his wife, 1835-1851, r.*
*Rev. John Newton, 1835-1891.
*Mrs. Elizabeth Newton, 1835-1857.
Mrs. Newton, 1866-1891, r.
Miss Julia Davis, 1835, r.*
Rev. James McEwen and his wife, 1836-1838, r.*
*Rev. James R. Campbell, 1836-1862.
*Mrs. James R. Campbell, 1836-1873.
Rev. Jesse M. Jamieson, 1836-1857, r.
*Mrs. Rebecca Jamieson, 1836-1845.
*Mrs. E. McL. Jamieson, 1848-1856.
*Rev. Joseph Porter, 1836-1853.
*Mrs. Porter, 1836-1842.
Rev. William S. Rogers and his wife, 1836-1843, r.*
Rev. Henry R. Wilson and his wife, 1838-1846, r.*
*Rev. John H. Morrison, 1838-1881.
*Mrs. Anna M. Morrison, died in Calcutta, April 27, 1838.
*Rev. Joseph Caldwell, 1838-1877.

---
† Colored.

APPENDICES.

*Mrs. Jane Caldwell, 1838-1839, Nov. 8th.
Mrs. Caldwell, 1842.
*Mr. James Craig, teacher, 1838-1845.
Mrs. J. Craig, 1838-1846, r.
Mr. Rees Morris, printer, and his wife, 1838-1845, r.

To Mission for China:
Rev. Robert Orr and his wife, 1838-1841, r.*
*Rev. John A. Mitchell, 1838.

Other missionaries of the Presbyterian Church were sent out by the American Board, in the years from 1832-1838, so far as recollected, viz.:

Rev. and Mrs. John B. Adger, to a Mediterranean field, r.
Rev. and Mrs. James R. Eckard, to Ceylon, r.*
Rev. Matthew B. Hope, to Singapore, r.*
Rev. J. Leighton and Mrs. Wilson, to Western Africa, r.*
Rev. W. M. Thomson, to Syria, 1833-1877, r.
*Mrs. Thomson, 1833-1873.
Rev. Elias Riggs, to Turkey, 1834-.
*Rev. Asher Wright, to Senecas, 1820-1875.
*Mrs. Wright, 1833-1886.
Rev. William Hall, 1834-.
*Mrs. Hall, 1834-1882.
*Rev. J. S. Williamson, M.D., to Dakotas, 1835-1879.
*Mrs. Williamson, 1835-1872.
Messrs. Thomson, Wright, Hall, and Williamson were received by transfer from the American Board in 1870.

II.

BOOKS OF REFERENCE.

GENERAL: The Assembly's Digest, 1820.
Dr. S. J. Baird's Digest G. A., second edition, 1858.
Minutes of the General Assembly, 1789-1840.
Minutes of the Synod of Pittsburgh, 1802-1832, printed in 1852.
Minutes, in manuscript, of the Board of Trust, 1804-1826.
Minutes, in manuscript, of the Western Foreign Missionary Society, 1831-1837.
Minutes, in manuscript, of the Board of Foreign Missions, 1837-1838.
Western Missionary Magazine, two vols., 1803-1805.
Foreign Missionary Chronicle, seventeen volumes, 1833-1850.
American Missionary Register, six volumes, 1817-1822. Z. Lewis, Esq., editor.
Sketches of Virginia and of North Carolina, and their Synods, containing in part, the Minutes of the Synods, two volumes, 1846, 1850, by Rev. W. H. Foote, D.D.
Old Redstone. Rev. Dr. J. Smith, 1854.
Presbyterian Centennial Convention, Pittsburgh, 1876, (with Missionary History of Rev. E. E. Swift, D.D.)
History of the Presbytery of Washington, 1889, by Rev. W. F. Hamilton, D.D. (Notices and portraits of missionaries; and Sketch of Missions, by Rev. W. H. Lester, D.D.)
Memoirs of Rev. David Brainerd. New York.
Memoirs of Rev. Elisha McCurdy, D.D., 1849, by Rev. David Elliott, D.D.

APPENDICES. 247

Historical Sketches of India Missions—Semi-Centennial. Allahabad Press, 1884.

Historical Sketches of Presbyterian Missions. Third edition, 1891, by Women's F. M. Society, Philadelphia.

Dr. J. Warren's Missionary Life in North India, 1862.

Mrs. H. H. Holcomb's Bits of Missionary Work in India, 1886.

SPECIAL—by missionaries, or relating to them, appointed from 1832–1838.

Memoir of the Rev. Joseph W. Barr, by Rev. E. P. Swift, D.D., 1833.

Memoir of Mrs. Louisa A. Lowrie, by Rev. A. G. Fairchild, D.D., 1834. London edition, with introduction on Woman's Work in Missions, by Rev. W. H. Pearce, 1835.

Memoir of Mrs. Anna M. Morrison, by Rev. Dr. E. J. Richards, New York, 1839.

Dictionary in Goormookhee, Sikh language, by Rev. John Newton, D.D. Lodiana Press.

The Bible translated into Goormookhee, Sikh language, and many tracts in Hindustani and other languages, by Rev. John Newton, D.D., and the other missionaries.

Missions in Hindustan, by Rev. J. R. Campbell, D.D. Philadelphia, 1852.

Travels in North India, Philadelphia, 1842. The same under the title of Two Years in Upper India, New York, 1850. Presbyterian Missions, New York; Third edition, 1868. Missionary Papers, New York, 1882. By Rev. John C. Lowrie.

The Land of Sinim, by Rev. Walter M. Lowrie.

INDEX OF SUPPLEMENTAL NOTES.

AFRICA, to Central via Liberia.................... 123
   Discouragements........ 124
   Doors opening........... 125
Agents, Collecting or Field. 187
Alexander, Rev. J. Addison, D.D.................. 183
Andrews, Rev. John....... 186

Books of reference........ 246
Bundelkhund, as a mission field................... 128

CALCUTTA, as a mission station.................... 182
   The purpose relinquished. 183
   Lessons learned.......... 131
   Missionaries and other friends................ 132
   Cordial intercourse among missionaries........... 132
   Interdenominational troubles, none............. 133
   Chief work of missionaries 135
   Exceptionable theories... 138
   Painful sights............ 139
Campbell, Rev. James R... 104
Chavis, Rev. John......... 7
Chinese metallic divisible types.................. 178
Christian union and co-operation, the true idea of.. 134
Cornplanter Indians, 1814, 1892................... 37

GREEN, Rev. Ashbel, D.D. vi

HERRON, Rev. Francis, D.D. 110

INDIA, population nearly 300,000,000; in deep ignorance as Pagans or Mohammedans; mostly in bondage to caste; some Anglo-Hindu students; Christian converts increasing; great changes; general outlook hopeful..131–140

LENOX, Mr. James......... 178
Lowrie, Hon. Walter...... 156

MAGAZINE, Western Missionary, 1803–1805....... 186
Missionary Chronicle, The Foreign, 1833–1850...... 184
McCurdy, Rev. Elisha, D.D. 75
McEwen, Rev. Jas. and Mrs. 165
Missions abroad, theory of. 96
Missions, United Foreign Society: Its plan of union; its pecuniary basis; how the Society ended; two things in its course..... 65–68
Missions, Synodical....... 69–82
   In Virginia.............. 69
   the Carolinas........... 69
   Western Pennsylvania and Ohio............. 72

INDEX OF SUPPLEMENTAL NOTES. 249

Missions, in Indian work... 73
   In Domestic work...... 75
   Itinerant usefulness.... 76
   Women's work, then and now............ 77
   A home-life incident... 77
   Great success.......... 82
   Lessons taught........ 82
Missions, Western Foreign Society; executive officers..............106–112
   Adverse action of G A... 201
   Sources of complete information................. 201
   Directors' circular letter.. 202
   Last minutes W. F. M. S. 214–220
   Its missions, property, etc., all transferred to the B. F. M........219, 220
   Final action of the G. A. 221–223
   The Board of Foreign Missions appointed........ 221
   Its constitution...... 221–223
   Its first meeting......... 226
   The missions and property of the Society transferred to the Board and accepted by it; also, later, the Central and Southern Boards; the city of New York chosen for the offices of the Board; a solemn acknowledgment of the favors and blessings of God, recorded; the Board adjourned....... 226
   The missionary discussions in the G. A. able and earnest, but not partisan, 224. The position, 225. Semi-annual meetings of the Board, not continued, 228.

PRESBYTERY of Lodiana... 148
Presbytery or "Mission"?.. 149

RAMMOHUN ROY, eminent in "comparative" Hindu learning................ 136

SOMÁJAS or Societies....... 136
Spurgeon's "I hate the science of comparative theology"................. 135
Sir Monier Williams, Dr. Chas. Hodge, our blessed Saviour, on such subjects. 136
Seneca and other Indian missions................ 50
Stuart, Mr. George H...... 164
Swift, Rev. Dr. E. P... 106, 202

WILSON and Newton, Rev. Messrs., and their families................147, 148
Wylie, Rev. Dr. T. W. J.... 614

www.ingramcontent.com/pod-product-compliance
Lightning Source LLC
Chambersburg PA
CBHW031350230426
43670CB00006B/494